Christianity and Social Issues

LIVING FAITH

MICHAEL KEENE

STANLEY THORNES (PUBLISHERS) LTD

LIVING FAITH:
Christianity and Social Issues

Other books in the series:

The Christian Experience
The Catholic Experience

> **Note:** Throughout the series BCE (Before Common or Christian Era) and CE (Common or Christian Era) have been used in place of the traditional BC and AD.

Text © Michael Keene 1995

Original illustrations © Stanley Thornes (Publishers) Ltd 1995

The rights of Michael Keene to be identified as author of this work has been asserted by him in accordance with the Copyright, Designs and Patents Act 1988

First published in 1995 by:
Stanley Thornes (Publishers) Ltd
Ellenborough House
Wellington Street
CHELTENHAM GL50 1YW
England

97 98 99 00 / 10 9 8 7 6 5 4 3 2

A catalogue record for this book is available from the British Library.

ISBN 0–7487–2190–8

Cover pictures used by permission of Zefa Pictures Ltd and Andes Press Agency/Carlos Reynes

Typeset in 11/13 Galliard and Stone

Produced by AMR Ltd for Stanley Thornes (Publishers) Ltd

Printed in Hong Kong

Acknowledgements

The publishers are grateful for permission to use copyright material, as follows:

Quotations from the Revised English Bible ©, by permission of Oxford University and Cambridge University Press 1989.

Also the following for permission to reproduce copyright photographs: *Andes Press Agency/Carlos Reyes:* pg 14, 56, 63, 83, 84, 89, 100, 101, 115, 128, 129, 132, 137, 140, 142, 144. *Colorific:* pg 17, 136. *Colorsport:* pg 50, 145. *Format:* pg 66 *Helen House, Oxford:* pg 104. *Hulton Deutsch:* pg 65, 82, 87, 119, 130. *Michael Keene:* pg 4, 7, 8, 12, 19, 26, 31, 40, 41, 42, 44, 48, 51, 52, 76, 80, 93, 113, 117, 120, 121, 124, 125, 127, 138, 139, 151. *LIFE:* pg 97. *Jo MacLennan and Alex Keene:* pg 5x2, 6x2, 9, 11, 13, 15, 18, 20, 21, 22, 23, 24, 25, 27, 28, 29, 30, 32, 34, 35, 36, 37, 38, 39, 40, 42, 45, 47, 53, 54, 55, 58, 59x2, 60, 61, 68, 69, 70, 72, 73, 74, 75, 77x2, 78, 79, 81, 91, 95, 98, 99, 102, 105, 106, 107, 112, 113, 116, 118, 125, 146, 148, 150. *Magnum Photo Library:* pg 48, 110, 133, 135, 141. *Mary Evans Picture Library:* pg 86, 126. *Oxford Scientific Library:* pg 94, 108. *Rex Features Ltd:* pg 10, 16, 33, 46, 62, 64, 90, 96, 114, 122, 123, 147, 149. *Science Photo Library:* pg 102, 111. *Sygma Photo Library:* pg 88, 92, 109.

The publishers have made every effort to trace the copyright holders, but if they have inadvertently overlooked any, they will be pleased to make the necessary arrangements at the first opportunity.

CONTENTS

1.1 WHO AM I?

It appears that human beings are pretty unimportant. Each one of us occupies a tiny fragment of space for a brief moment of time. We come and go barely being noticed and our impact upon the planet is negligible. Within a few years of our deaths we are hardly even remembered. A grim picture, maybe, but that is how it seems. Is that, however, how you see it?

The Bible offers a very different picture of the human race as these two quotations make clear:

a) "God created human beings in his own image; in the image of God he created them…" (Genesis 1.27)

b) "…what is a frail mortal, that you should be mindful of him, a human being, that you should take notice of him? Yet you have made him a little less than a god…" (Psalm 8.4,5)

The Bible insists that there are two sides to the picture. On the one hand, human life on earth is as grass blossoming 'like a wild flower in the meadow' until the wind passes over us and we are gone (Psalm 103.15). On the other hand, we have been created in the Divine image and are almost god-like. We have been given great gifts, and great responsibilities to go with them. These lift us far above all other forms of life. We are 'stewards', God's representatives on earth, given the awesome task of looking after the planet. It is a responsibility for which we will be held to account at some time in the future. That is the Bible's assessment.

The learning process

We begin the learning process the moment we are born. Our earliest learning experiences take place within our family.

A *Without a care in the world – yet what responsibility for the world in which she lives is this little girl going to carry in the future?*

It is there that we learn how to:

1 relate to other people;
2 love others and be loved by them;
3 carry responsibility;
4 deal with our anger and frustration;
5 be a good friend.

As we grow, so our circle of friends begins to expand. We come to realise that we are part of a much larger 'family'. In that family we discover the 'roles' that we are expected to play in the future as a son or daughter; as a brother or sister; as a husband or wife and as a father or mother. Our grandparents, school teachers, parents, brothers and sisters, friends and the mass media (radio, television, etc) all become our teachers. They play their part in a process which never ends. We never stop learning.

What about religion?

Religion plays an important part in the lives of some young people. They go with their parents to the local church, synagogue or mosque. They are taught certain 'truths' about God and about themselves. These 'truths' include the following:

a) That God created the universe, the earth and every human being.
b) That each human being is unique and important. No two people are exactly the same.
c) That everyone is made up of two parts – the physical (their body) and the spiritual (their soul). It is the soul which enables us to worship God.

To religious people the soul is more important than the body. We can never know or appreciate ourselves until we come to know our spiritual capabilities. Some people attain this religious outlook later in life. Others, however, may live the whole of their lives without giving any thought to their capacity for worshipping God.

One important point. Our outlook on life has a considerable effect on the way that we live. It makes a marked difference to the way that we look at ourselves and the ways that we treat other people. This is something that you may like to spend some time thinking about.

ANSWER IN YOUR BOOK ...

1 What does the Bible teach us about the importance of human beings?

2 What is a 'role'?

3 What do the different religions teach us about God and human beings?

DISCUSS AMONG YOURSELVES ...

a) How many different 'roles' can you list that you are expected to play at the moment? Cover all areas of your life, home, school, church, etc, as well as your different social activities and relationships with friends.

b) Compare your list with that of two other people in your class. To what extent do your lists agree? What are the differences?

c) How do you work out your responsibilities in these different roles? Take three of the roles that you are playing at the moment and list five responsibilities which you have in each role.

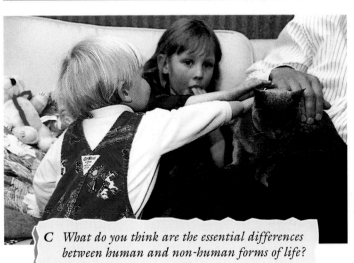

C What do you think are the essential differences between human and non-human forms of life?

B What responsibilities do you think young and old people have towards each other?

WHAT DO YOU THINK?

The religious approach emphasises that all human beings have physical and spiritual dimensions: the latter being by far the most important.

a) Do you think that there are two, or more, aspects to human nature? How would you describe each one of them?

b) What do you think are the limits placed on human beings? Is there anything to stop human beings doing just as they please?

c) Do you think that this life is all that there is? Is there anything about human life which leads you to suspect that there may be something beyond our present existence?

IN THE GLOSSARY ...

Mass Media; Bible; Soul.

1.2 RELATIONSHIPS

One of the first lessons we learn in life is that none of us live in splendid isolation. John Donne, the poet, was surely right when he wrote:

> "No man is an island, entire of itself."

From the moment we were conceived we began to form a very close relationship with our mother in her womb. The relationship was one of total dependency. After our birth the relationship became even closer. At the same time we began to form dependent relationships with other people, especially our father. We responded to them and enjoyed having them respond to us.

A *A baby's first relationship. Why do you think this relationship is so important both for the baby and the mother?*

Different relationships

So the process begins. Throughout our life we are going to form relationships with many different people in a whole variety of ways. These relationships can be divided into two clear groups:

a) *Primary relationships.* These are the relationships that form the basis of our lives. To begin with they centre around our family. They then expand to include our friends and later include our relationship with our husband or wife and our new family. These are likely to be the closest relationships that any of us form. They will arouse very strong feelings within both us and other people. This means that they have the potential to do one of two things. They can either make an unrivalled contribution to our happiness or have the opposite effect. If they work they will bring great joy into our lives. If they fail they will cause us great distress.

b) *Secondary relationships.* There will always be people who play an important, but not central, part in our lives. Some will touch our lives for a while and then move on. Others stay longer but remain on the fringes of our experience.

Each relationship makes its own demands on us. For instance, our relationship with our parents makes very different demands to those relationships we have with our friends. Relationships also change as time goes by. When we are young our parents provide us with our sense of identity and security. Later on, however, we may find those ingredients elsewhere. This can be a problem. Both parents and children often find it difficult to adjust to changing conditions. You may be able to come up with a few examples of this.

Changing relationships

Let us look back to our earliest relationships for a moment. A new-born baby is totally dependent on its parents to be changed and fed. Even at an early age, however, it

B *We know how a mother forms a close bond with her baby but how does a father do this? Is it just as important that he does?*

C Why have these boys formed such a close bond with each other? Why is this important?

All real adult relationships have to be ones of inter-dependence. Only then can the marks of a real friendship – love, trust, caring and respect – grow. People must always have the freedom to grow and express themselves. Mature friendships also need to change. Just as we change continually, so do our relationships with other people. This is the only way to reach maturity. Change may not always be comfortable or pleasant but it is essential. This is something that we should always bear in mind.

will find ways of making its needs known. This is something you can ask any parent! It is only when it learns to crawl, and then walk, that it struggles towards some measure of independence. While it will be many years before it can be totally independent, even at this early age, the relationship between child and parent is changing. It is becoming one of inter-dependence rather than dependence.

ANSWER IN YOUR BOOK ...

1 What is a primary relationship?
2 What is a secondary relationship?
3 What are the marks of a mature, adult relationship?

IN YOUR OWN WORDS ...

a) Describe the difference between primary and secondary relationships.

b) Describe two primary relationships in your life. Why are these relationships particularly important? How do you expect them to change as you get older?

c) Describe two secondary relationships which you have? Why are most secondary relationships only passing? What do you think we all gain from the many secondary relationships that we have with others?

CAN YOU EXPLAIN?

When Jesus was asked by one of the Pharisees which of the many commandments in the Jewish law was the most important he replied that there were two relationships which really mattered. The first was to love God with our entire being and the second was to love our neighbour as ourselves (Matthew 22.39).
Answer the following questions:

a) What are we saying if we describe these two relationships as 'primary'?

b) What do you think it means in practice to love God and to love our neighbour?

c) Why do you think that Jesus linked loving God with loving ourselves and our neighbour?

IN THE GLOSSARY ...

Primary Relationships; Secondary Relationships.

1.3 FRIENDSHIP

In this chapter we will look more closely at friendship. Our first friends were almost certainly drawn from those around us in our family such as our brothers, sisters, cousins, etc. Our parents then made it possible for us to draw friends from a wider circle – from children living next door, down our street or from our immediate locality. We were not aware of it, of course, but these friends were usually chosen for us quite carefully!

The choice only really became ours when we started at school although even then, the teacher was probably 'arranging' things quite carefully behind the scenes! Some of the friendships struck up at this time have turned out to be very strong and remained with us ever since. Others, though, have not survived. What do you think you have learned from these friendships, whether they have survived or not? Did they play an important part in your growth and development?

Where do our friends come from?

The business of choosing friends is not quite as haphazard as you might think. Although, in theory, we can choose our friends from anywhere it is most likely that they will:

a) *Come from a similar background to us.* Most of our early friends, for instance, come from our own area.
b) *Go to the same club, organisation or church as us.* We have to meet our friends somewhere and a casual setting like a club is a likely meeting place. They may, of course, go to our school.
c) *Share interests with us.* Friends like being together and often have a common interest which binds them closely.
d) *Share some of our beliefs and opinions.* Most friendships which grow into lasting relationships build upon what they have in common. Obviously, this does not mean that friends have to be 'clones' of each other. In a good friendship, there is plenty of room for differences.

Destroying a friendship

Friendships do not always last. All of them come under strain from time to time. If they withstand the pressure

A *Friendship is the same the world over. Why is it likely to be very important in the lives of these girls?*

they usually become stronger as a result. Sometimes, though, they do not. People often move to a different area or they simply grow apart. Often, however, the break-up is more traumatic. Perhaps the friends start to compete with each other or there is a misunderstanding between them. Maybe one friend grows jealous of the other and envies his or her looks, possessions, talents, achievements, etc. The problem is that once hurtful words are said and a break made, it is very difficult to repair the damage this can do to a friendship.

None of this should surprise us. Exactly the same thing happens in friendships between adults. It certainly happened frequently among the early Christians. As the number of Christian communities grew, so did the number of bitter disputes. Some of the disputes were fundamental. Within a few years of the death of Jesus, for instance, the Church was split right down the middle over whether non-Jews (Gentiles) should be compelled to live like Jews when they became Christians. This argument was fuelled by the fact that most of the early Christians were Jews.

B Friendship obviously matters – no matter what age people are. What do you think that these elderly people are looking for in their friendships with each other?

The early Christians recognised that even close friends were likely to fall out over such issues so they developed a simple procedure for dealing with disagreements. (Refer to READ AND DECIDE...)

Although these words have probably been attributed to Jesus by later believers, they do reflect the way that people behaved in the early Church. As you will also discover, Paul had his own advice for dealing with such disagreements.

ANSWER IN YOUR BOOK ...

1 How do most of us make friends?

2 What factors can put a strain on a friendship?

3 What is the Biblical advice for dealing with quarrels and disagreements within any relationship? (Consult READ AND DECIDE...)

READ AND DECIDE ...

These are two ways suggested in the New Testament for dealing with quarrels and disagreements:

a) **Matthew 18.15-17:**
"If your brother does wrong, go and take the matter up with him, strictly between yourselves. If he listens to you, you have won your brother over. But if he will not listen, take one or two others with you, so that every case may be settled on the evidence of two or three witnesses. If he refuses to listen to them, report the matter to the congregation; and if he will not listen even to the congregation, then treat him as you would a pagan or a tax-collector..."

b) **Ephesians 4.26:**
"If you are angry, do not be led into sin; do not let sunset find you nursing your anger..."

Do you think that either of these verses have anything important to say about disagreements arising within a friendship. Give reasons for your answer.

WRITE AN ESSAY ...

The Bible has a lot to say about friendship. Look up each of the following references and make your own notes.

a) Proverbs 7.17

b) Proverbs 18.24

c) Proverbs 27.17

d) John 15.13

Now write an essay with the title:
'What is friendship and why does it matter?'

IN THE GLOSSARY ...

Church; Jew; Paul; Gentile.

1.4 RIGHT AND WRONG

Before we get very far in the process of growing up we find ourselves up against one of the greatest problems in life. How do we tell the difference between right and wrong? Even a young child discovers that life is full of situations which demand that such a choice is made:

1 Should I admit what I have done or try to get away with it?
2 Is it always necessary to tell the truth or can I be economical with it sometimes?
3 What should my reaction be when someone is unkind or hurts me?

The same moral dilemmas, in a different form, also confront adults. Moral decision-making is a constant struggle. The situations which prompt the questions may change but the questions themselves return time and time again to haunt us.

It is a fact of life that both child and adult find it far from easy to work out the 'right' thing to do. The water is, of course, muddied considerably if we know the 'right' thing to do but find that it conflicts with what we really 'want' to do. A tussle then develops between our knowledge of what is right and our 'conscience'. Our 'conscience' seems to be a part of us that develops out of the many influences that affect us, although many Christians see their consciences as being the 'voice of God'. These influences include the following:

❖ *Our parents.* In the process of bringing us up, our parents indicate what they consider to be right and wrong. When we are young we take their ideas on board without giving them serious consideration. It is only when we get older that questions begin to arise.
❖ *The example of others.* The influence of people that we respect can be considerable. We may talk matters over with them or simply be aware of what they would do in a similar situation.
❖ *Our own experience.* We may have seen what has happened to other people faced with a similar decision or have been confronted with it ourselves on a previous occasion. Very often, this experience enables us to see the difference between right and wrong.

❖ *Our rules.* All of us follow certain rules to help us live our lives. Those rules may be adopted from our parents, come from our faith in God or be broadly similar to those adopted by our friends. We may also follow the moral teachings of a particular Church.
❖ *Our feelings.* When we have to make major decisions, our feelings often play a large part in how we decide. Sometimes, we just know something to be wrong even if we cannot precisely say why.

A Why do you think that the vast majority of people would say that it is wrong to burgle someone else's property?

Making up our minds

Christians are often required to make moral decisions in the course of their everyday life. Within the Christian Church there are, broadly speaking, two very different approaches to the problem:

a) *The Roman Catholic approach.* Roman Catholics believe that God has revealed himself and his will through the Holy Scriptures, Tradition and the Pope. This has allowed the will of God to be known on such controversial issues as contraception, abortion and euthanasia. Knowledge of the Divine will has been channelled through the Church. To go against the teaching of the Church on such matters is, therefore, to go against the will of God.

b) *The Protestant approach.* Protestants look to the Bible, the 'Word of God', for the answers to their moral questions. Sometimes the Bible seems to provide a direct answer as it does, for example, on the issue of homosexuality. More often, however, Protestants look for principles in the Bible which could be applied to the issue they are considering.

B *How do you think this young Christian might use the Bible in helping her to decide between what is right and what is wrong? What do you think are the advantages and disadvantages of using this approach?*

ANSWER IN YOUR BOOK ...

1 What do you think the 'conscience' is?

2 What is the Roman Catholic approach to the problem of deciding between right and wrong?

3 What is the Protestant approach to deciding between right and wrong?

WHAT DO YOU THINK?

a) How do you think that young children begin to work out the difference between right and wrong? What part do you think 'rules' play in these early decisions? Where do most of these rules come from?

b) Do you think that 'feelings' have an important part to play in this decision-making process or not? Can you provide any examples of situations where a person might legitimately 'feel' that something is right even though it is clearly wrong?

c) Do you think that other people can, or should, play a part in our deciding between right or wrong?

d) What has been the major influence in helping you to decide the difference between right and wrong?

USE YOUR IMAGINATION ...

The Ten Commandments (Exodus 20) are the most famous code of laws. Imagine that you are a Protestant who wishes to understand the 'spirit' of the Commandments and their relevance to life today. How do you think the Commandments might be applied to the following problems:

a) War and violence.

b) Elderly people and the way they are treated.

c) Euthanasia.

d) Adultery and sexual activity outside marriage.

e) Pollution and looking after the environment.

IN THE GLOSSARY ...

Roman Catholic Church; Protestant; Holy Scriptures; Pope; Abortion; Birth-control; Contraception; Euthanasia; Bible; Homosexual.

1.5 LOVE

In recent years the word 'love' has been vastly over-used. We now use it to describe a wide range of experiences. We may love plum jam; a singer, actor or actress; our parents, brothers and sisters; our pet and our boyfriend or girlfriend. Some of us may speak of our love for God. The same word – but a wide variety of meanings.

Centuries ago, the Greeks faced a similar problem and introduced four different words to express the many different meanings. They spoke of:

1 *eros* – a love which is based upon a simple physical attraction and from which we gain the word 'erotic';
2 *philos* – a love for those close to us, our family and friends;
3 *storge* – the warm affection that we may have for a particular place;
4 *agape (Christian love)* – a reflection of the love that God has for us. It includes loving people to whom we do not feel attracted; people who do not respond to us and even people that we do not like.

We can say that there are two extremes to love:

a) The 'lust' which takes place when we try to 'possess' someone else (eros). We then use them as an outlet for our own sexual desires. Lust is totally selfish.
b) A pure, selfless love by which we place ourselves totally at the service of others (agape).

Jesus left his disciples in little doubt as to exactly what he meant by love. He told them that they must put the needs of others before their own without looking for any return on their love. As Jesus stated in the collection of sayings known as the 'Sermon on the Mount' (Matthew 5-7):

> "If you love only those who love you what reward can you expect? ...There must be no limit to your goodness, as your heavenly father's goodness knows no bounds." (Matthew 5.46-48)

That is real love!

The most well-known and important description of 'love' in the New Testament comes from Paul. Writing to the Christians in Corinth he described the characteristics of true love in this way:

A This is a very special love but how would you describe it?

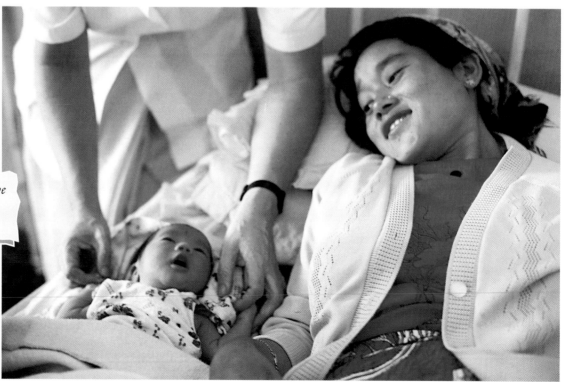

12

"Love is patient and kind. Love envies no one, is never boastful, never conceited, never rude; love is never selfish, never quick to take offence. Love keeps no score of wrongs, takes no pleasure in the sins of others but delights in the truth. There is nothing love cannot face; there is no limit to its faith, its hope, its endurance. Love will never come to an end..." (1.Corinthians 13.4-8)

B This is a very special kind of love but how would you describe it? What have this couple given to each other over many years? How do you think a love like this lasts and grows?

ANSWER IN YOUR BOOK ...

1 Which four words did the Greek use for love? What did they mean by them?

2 What is unique about Christian love – agape?

3 Summarise, in your own words, Paul's description of love in 1.Corinthians 13. What do you think are the most striking and important phrases in the description? Can you write a similar description which sums up what people feel about love today?

READ AND DECIDE ...

Here are three quotations from the New Testament about love. Read them carefully:

a) "...if someone says, 'I love God', while at the same time hating his fellow-Christian, he is a liar. If he does not love a fellow-Christian whom he has seen, he is incapable of loving God whom he has not seen." (1.John 4.20)

b) "Live in love as Christ loved you and gave himself up on your behalf, an offering and sacrifice whose fragrance is pleasing to God." (Ephesians 5,2)

c) "This is my commandment: love one another, as I have loved you. There is no greater love than this, that someone should lay down his life for his friends." (John 15.12,13)

Each of these quotations makes an important point about love. Describe, in your own words, what it is.

WHAT DO YOU THINK?

Read Matthew 5.43,44. Now answer these questions:

a) Have you recently had an argument with someone? If so, how did you react? How did the conflict end? Did you find it difficult/impossible to love your 'enemy' in that situation? What do you think might have happened if you had tried to follow the instructions of Jesus?

b) What do you think Jesus meant here by your 'enemy'?

c) Do you think that people can be commanded to 'love'?

d) What is distinctive about Christian love?

DISCUSS AMONG YOURSELVES ...

Here are two quotations for you to talk about:

a) **Dorothy Parker:**
"Love is like quicksilver in the hand. Leave the fingers open and it stays. Clutch it and it darts away."

b) **W.B.Yeats:**
"It is love that I am seeking for
But of a beautiful unheard-of kind
That is not in the world."

IN THE GLOSSARY ...

Sermon on the Mount; Paul.

1.6 FAMILY LIFE

In our society the family is the most important social unit. The exact form that it takes may vary but it is found almost everywhere and seems to meet the needs of people better than any other arrangement. The family unit can take one of two forms.

The extended family

This is the form of family life found throughout the Bible. It is still found in many countries today. In an extended family several generations of the same family either live together in the same house or within a very short distance of each other. Grandparents, parents and children, not to mention aunts and uncles, are close together so that they can support and help each other whenever the need arises. This is essential in many societies where the State does not help to look after the very young or the very old.

The extended family is mainly found in agricultural societies. As soon as people move away from the area to study or work the extended family breaks up. It was found to be prospering in working-class areas of the U.K., such as the East End of London and Manchester, until the 1950s. Today, however, it is not practised very often in this country.

The nuclear family

In the modern Western family children often leave home around the age of eighteen to go to college or find work. They rarely return home afterwards. When they, in turn, marry and set up a home it contains just two generations – parents and children. Grandparents may well be some distance away and

contact is only maintained through infrequent visits and family get-togethers for Christmas and birthdays.

There is a world of difference between these two types of family. In one, the extended arrangement, parents have the benefit of advice and help from the older generation in bringing up their children. The links between the different generations is a close one and older family members feel valued for their advice and wisdom. In a nuclear family, grandparents contribute little to the next generation.

Other forms of family life

About 50% of people in the U.K. live in a nuclear family. The remainder live in a variety of alternative family arrangements:

1 *An expanded family.* Old people, the disabled or the mentally handicapped sometimes live together as a family and help to look after one another.
2 *A community.* Some people choose to live together and share work, childcare and property. Others, such as monks and nuns, live together in a religious community.

A *This extended family comes from South Africa. What do you think are the advantages and disadvantages of belonging to an extended family?*

14

3 *A reconstituted family.* Divorced people who re-marry often bring children with them into their new relationship. As a result, two families are combined and brought up together.

4 *A single-parent family.* A family in which one parent is left to bring up the children on their own. This will be discussed further in Unit 1.8.

5 *A childless family.* One in every ten married couples cannot have children because one or other of them is infertile (unable to conceive). Some married couples choose not to have a family and many couples have grown-up children who have left home.

Why is the family important?

Many people, including most Christians, feel that the family is very important. They point out that the family does the following:

a) Gives us our sense of identity. This includes our history, name, physical characteristics, values and opinions.

b) Teaches us how we are expected to behave (a process called 'socialisation'). This prepares us for the role we will play in society as an adult.

c) Provides our first really close bonding with others. From this we learn how to give and receive love; how to deal with our feelings; how to treat others with care and consideration and how to share.

d) Provides the best way of caring for the very young and, in some cases, the very old as well.

It has to be taken into consideration that all of this only applies to the most perfect of families. Very few families live up to all of these ideals. Modern psychiatry shows that many problems and difficulties encountered in later years can be traced back to early family life. Family life can be enormously creative and positive but it can also be very destructive.

WHAT DO YOU THINK?

The photograph of the nuclear family shows what most people today understand by a family. The real situation, however, is rather more complicated.

a) Look again at the list of other 'forms' of family life. Do they all fit in with your idea of what makes up a 'family'? Are there any that you feel unhappy about?

b) Why do you think that some married couples choose not to have children? Does the idea appeal to you? Give reasons for your answer. What do you think couples gain or lose by not having children of their own?

c) If you discovered that you or your partner were infertile what would you do? Would you try to adopt a child or go through life without children? Can you explain the reasons for your answer?

ANSWER IN YOUR BOOK ...

1 What is an extended family?

2 What is a nuclear family?

3 Why is family life important?

READ AND DECIDE ...

We know very little about the family life of Jesus. One incident recorded in the Gospels, however, is worth looking at closely. Read Mark 3.31-35 through carefully.

a) Is Jesus rejecting his family here?

b) If so, why?

c) If not, what point is he trying to make?

B Why do you think that most people find the nuclear family better suited to modern life than the extended family? Do you think that we have lost anything important by moving from one to the other?

IN THE GLOSSARY ...

Extended Family; Nuclear Family; Monk; Nun; One-parent Family; Socialisation.

1.7 ALTERNATIVES TO FAMILY LIFE

From time to time groups of people have tried to develop alternatives to family life. Some groups have tried to drop out of conventional life completely and develop their own particular approach to living together and having children. One of the problems that they have found is that of convincing other members of society to accept them for what they are. Rarely have these attempts been successful.

During this century two attempts have been made on a much larger scale to develop alternative forms of family life. They both question the human race's habit of dividing up into small family groups.

The Russian Experiment

After the Russian Revolution in 1917, some of the revolutionaries tried to abolish traditional Russian family life. They argued that most of the time which people spent performing household chores was wasted. If people lived in communes and shared out the tasks everybody, including the country itself, would benefit. The Russian leader Lenin stated:

> "The home life of a woman is a daily sacrifice to a thousand unimportant trivialities."

To replace them collectives were set up to look after child-care, kitchen work, laundry services, etc, freeing women to return quickly to full-time work. The marriage laws were rewritten to give women equal rights with men and divorce was made easier.

The experiment was not a success. The revolutionaries had underestimated the amount of work that each family actually does. The State collectives were unable to meet all the needs of the children. Making divorce easier was intended to free women from the shackles of an unworkable marriage. In fact, it allowed men to walk out more easily, leaving women and children without any means of support.

The Israeli Kibbutz

The modern state of Israel was founded in 1948. Soon after this a new form of communal living was introduced – the kibbutz. The idea was to raise the country's agricultural production by introducing collective farms – the kibbutzim. The people who work on these farms receive little or no pay. They share out the tasks. Some may work on the farm, some work in the factory, some help in the kitchens and some look after other workers' children.

The workers have few personal possessions. From the kibbutz they receive board and lodging, healthcare, childcare and education. If people want to live together they do not need to go through any formal wedding ceremony. Instead, they simply change a single room for a double one. When children are born they are brought up by trained staff in the Children's Home.

The heyday of the kibbutzim has passed. When they were first introduced some 10% of Israel's population worked on them but that figure is now down to less than 3%. Recent generations of children born and

A *A travellers camp. Do you find this way of life attractive or do you look on travellers as being totally irresponsible?*

brought up on them have argued that they wanted and needed some form of family life with their own possessions and privacy. Communal living was not able to meet their personal needs.

ANSWER IN YOUR BOOK ...

1 Why does society find it difficult to come to terms with those who want to adopt a different pattern of life?

2 What pattern of family life was introduced after the Russian revolution in 1917 and why did it fail?

3 What was unique about the Israeli attempt to increase agricultural production through its kibbutzim?

WHAT DO YOU THINK?

The kibbutz system has been the most well-known modern attempt to replace the narrow, exclusiveness of family life. Think about these questions carefully and discuss them among yourselves:

a) What do you think was the initial attractiveness of the kibbutz? Why do you think that many foreigners spent some months working on the communal farms? What was the attraction for them?

b) Look at the experiment from the point of view of the parents and their children for a moment. What do you think parents gained and lost from living on a kibbutz? What do you think children gained and lost from being a part of the same experiment?

c) Do you think there can be a successful and popular alternative to family life. If so, what form do you think it might take?

B An Israeli kibbutz. Why do you think this experiment in communal living was set up in the first place?

READ AND DECIDE ...

St Paul had a communal aspect very much in mind when he wrote these words about the Church:

> "For just as in a single human body there are many limbs and organs, all with different functions, so we who are united with Christ, though many, form one body, and belong to one another as its limbs and organs." (Romans 12.4,5)

This extract gives you a flavour of just what Paul had in mind. Read Romans 12.4-8 to get the whole idea. In what ways do these ideas match those behind a commune or a kibbutz?

1.8 SINGLE-PARENT FAMILIES

There are now over 1,200,000 'single-parent' families in the U.K., representing 5% of all families in this country. Perhaps the 'typical' family with two parents is not so typical after all! In over 80% of these one-parent families, it is the mother who has been left to bring up the children on her own.

Consider these facts for a moment:

a) In 1971 the number of single-parent families in the U.K. was 620,000 and in 1976, 750,000. In the last 15 years this number has increased by over 35% and it is still going up.
b) Over 1,600,000 children in the U.K. under the age of 16 are now being brought up by a single-parent. Of this number, 1,300,000 are living with their mother and 300,000 with their father. Almost everyone in this group finds themselves living in poverty and hardship.

Why are there so many single-parents?

There are several reasons why a single-parent family may come into existence:

1 A woman becomes pregnant but cannot, or does not wish to, marry the child's father. She rejects abortion and decides to bring the child up herself. It is a brave decision to make but one that will present many difficulties.
2 The husband or wife dies while there are still young children in the family. In this case, it is more likely to be the father who dies and the mother who is left to bring up the family.
3 The husband or wife deserts his or her partner and leaves them to bring up the children.
4 The parents divorce or separate and one (usually the mother) is given custody of the children. One in every three marriages now end in divorce and in a high number of these, children under the age of 16 are involved. The majority of one-parent families come from this group.

Problems for single parents

The vast majority of single parents are likely to face real difficulties. Some, of course, receive help and support from their family and friends but the vast majority have to struggle with all the pressures on their own. There are many practical problems:

a) If they want to work full-time they have to find, and pay for, someone to look after their child/children in working hours. In some parts of the U.K., creches are available for working mothers but in other parts, these are almost non existent. There is also a lack of trained child-minders.
b) If single-parents do not work they have to rely on State benefits to survive. These are barely sufficient. Recent surveys suggest that over 90% of non-working single mothers in the U.K. are living in poverty.

A *Three children to bring up and no-one to share the responsibility with. What problems do you think this single parent has?*

c) In those cases where fathers are liable to pay maintenance the money is often not paid or comes irregularly. There was much concern in the U.K. in 1994 over the activities of the CSA (Child Support Agency), which was set up to compel absent fathers to pay maintenance to their ex-wives and families.

To help single parents in the U.K. cope with some of these difficulties, several organisations have been set up. Perhaps the most well-known of these is the Gingerbread Association for one-parent families.

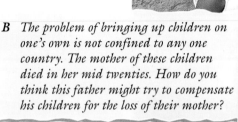

B *The problem of bringing up children on one's own is not confined to any one country. The mother of these children died in her mid twenties. How do you think this father might try to compensate his children for the loss of their mother?*

ANSWER IN YOUR BOOK ...

1 How many single-parent families are there in the U.K?

2 Why are there so many single-parent families? Why has the number increased so rapidly in recent years?

3 What are the main problems faced by single parents?

4 Do you think that single fathers face exactly the same problems as single mothers in trying to bring up a family on their own? Do they each have their own set of problems?

WHAT DO YOU THINK?

Here is a comment from Jackie, aged 15. Read it through carefully and try to imagine the situation out of which the comment came:

"My parents got divorced two years ago. Before that they argued all the time. Life in our house was hell. Now my Mum and I can get on with our own lives in peace. She gets tired after work but I help her in the house. Some of my friends feel sorry for me – but I'm happier now than I have ever been."

a) Do you think that a child always needs two parents? Give reasons for your answer.

b) Is one happy parent better than two unhappy ones? Explain your answer.

COMPLETE A CHART ...

What is life really like for a child growing up in a one-parent situation? Could there be any advantages? What are likely to be the main disadvantages? Draw up your own list in the form of a chart:

Advantages	Disadvantages
1	
2	
3	

IN THE GLOSSARY ...

One-parent Family; Abortion; Separation.

2.1 SEXUAL RELATIONSHIPS

Our sexual drive (libido) plays a part in our lives from the moment we are born. It is not until we reach adolescence, however, that it begins to arouse some very strong emotions – frustration, love, anger, pleasure, lust, hate, desire and revulsion – within us. We soon discover that sex involves far more than physical sensations alone. It also involves very deep feelings. It changes people.

A For a time, simple but satisfying contact between two people may be enough. How does a relationship go on from there?

Sexual contact

There are a number of levels at which physical contact between men and women take place:

1 *Through sight, hearing or smell*. Initially, our interest in someone of the opposite sex is aroused in this way. Why do we take so much care with the way we dress or with the deodorant or perfume that we wear?
2 *Through touch*. An arm around the shoulders or holding hands are initial signs of affection. They also show that two people have 'paired off' and are interested in developing a relationship with each other.
3 *Through kissing*. This may be a simple peck on the cheek, followed by a deeper and more meaningful kiss on the lips. Kissing someone lovingly is a very personal thing to do.
4 *Through intimate touching*. The bare body, especially breasts, and the sexual organs. This arouses both the man and the woman quickly. Their bodies are now ready for a deep sexual involvement.

5 *Through sexual intercourse*. There are three important points to be made about sexual contact:

a) Sexual arousal is intended to be progressive. You first become interested in someone else through your senses – the shape of their body, the sound of their voice or the scent that they are wearing. This progresses through touching and successive stages of intimacy to full sex.
b) Each of these steps involves a different level of arousal. It is much easier to draw back when the level of arousal is low. It becomes much more difficult to do this when a high level of arousal is involved. Once the sexual organs have been aroused, 'holding back' requires a great deal of self-control.
c) When two people are attracted towards each other a measure of commitment is involved. It might begin with common interests and friendship but this leads to 'going steady', falling in love, engagement and, possibly, marriage. Most people would say that there should be a strong link between the degree of commitment which two people feel towards each other and the extent of their sexual involvement. What do you think they mean when they say this?

These matters will be considered more fully in Unit 2.2. Here we make just one simple point. Questions about sex arise when we reach puberty, the stage which lies between childhood and adulthood. Puberty is a time when important changes take place in our bodies. It is also a time when our emotions and interests change as well. For most young people it is a time of confusion and uncertainty. Our bodies may reach full sexual maturity but very few, if any of us, are ready for a full-scale sexual relationship. To a certain extent the law recognises this. It has made sexual relationships under the age of 16 illegal. Because sex from the age of 16 onwards is legal, it does not follow that it is wise or sensible. How do you think a young person is able to tell when sexual involvement and commitment is sensible for them?

B How far do you think a relationship between a couple should go without any real love and commitment being involved?

ANSWER IN YOUR BOOK ...

1 What are the different levels of sexual contact between two people?

2 How does sexual arousal work?

3 What is the link between sexual arousal and commitment?

WHAT DO YOU THINK?

A widely quoted opinion on sex comes from Mary Calderone, an American sociologist:

"A girl plays at sex for which she is not ready because fundamentally what she wants is love; and a boy plays at love, for which he is not ready, because what he wants is sex."

Do you think that men and women have very different attitudes to sex as this quote suggests? If so, how? Do you think that many problems arise in relationships simply because the two sexes do not understand each other?

DISCUSS AMONG YOURSELVES ...

Sex education is a very controversial issue. Form yourselves into small groups and consider each of the following questions:

a) What should parents tell their children about sex education at home? When should they tell them?

b) What do you think about sex education in schools? Should it take place at all? At what age should it begin? What should it include? Is there anything that should not be included?

c) How would you assess the sex education that you have received? Has it prepared you for the future? Can you suggest any ways in which it might have been improved?

d) A strong movement in the U.S.A. has been formed to campaign for celibacy (abstaining from sex) in young people until they marry. In some parts of the U.S.A., this teaching is now part of school sex education programmes. Do you think this is good advice to give to young people today?

IN THE GLOSSARY ...

Puberty; Adolescence.

2.2 SEX AND RESPONSIBILITY

It's a basic fact of life that every form of life must reproduce to survive. It is as true for the human race as it is for any other species. The Biblical story of creation recognises this when God orders the first man and woman to:

> "Be fruitful and increase, fill the earth …"
> (Genesis 1.28)

For every form of life but one, sexual activity or mating is concerned with reproduction alone. The one exception is the human race. Human beings alone, it seems, find sex a pleasurable activity in its own right. Contraception (birth-control) allows couples to separate making love from the simple need to create new life.

Sex outside marriage

Until quite recently, most people agreed that the only suitable place for sex was within marriage. They did so primarily because they were frightened of conceiving a baby 'out of wedlock' (outside marriage). In the Victorian period many pregnant girls were sent away from home because of the disgrace they had brought upon the family. This fear guided their sexual behaviour. Nowadays, however, this fear can be largely removed by the responsible use of birth-control.

For many people sex is a very special activity. It is a unique way for two people to express their love for each other. This can only be the case if both of them are acting responsibly towards each other and towards anyone else who may be affected by what they are doing. That rules out 'casual sex'.

What about the argument over sex 'inside' and sex 'outside' marriage? Many people in a sexual relationship believe that they are acting responsibly, even though they are not married. In certain situations there are some Christians who would agree with them. The Christian Church as a whole, however, is firmly on the side of those who argue that the only really suitable place for sexual intercourse is within marriage. It makes the following points:

a) Sex is a God-given activity which demands total commitment and trust if it is to be really meaningful. For this to happen both partners must feel totally secure and such security can only be found within a marriage.

A *The mass media (newspaper, television, films, etc) bombard us with 'messages' about sex. Can you list some of these 'messages'? Do you think that these 'messages' have a great impact on the way we behave?*

Teenage thoughts on food, drugs and sex

Plea for more aid for young sex offenders

Cadet leader had sex with girl, 14

Sex claims totally untrue, dean tells congregation

Families cleared of sex abuse go home to their shattered lives

Legalise sex for sale, say nurses

Pope condemns 'rampant porn'

TV porn channel wins UK licence

Lone woman pilot 'endured endless sexual taunts'

Doctor made 'honest error' on abortions

Sex-case Pc cleared for sex

Police 'smash multi-million pornography ring'

Cardinal silent on sex claims

Boy blames father's death mother's affair

Runaway 'slaves' tell of sex abuse and attacks

Tribunal backs decision to sack sex-pest lecturer

Children's claims of sexual abuse 'drew on videos'

I'm not an adulterer, Dean tells cathedral

"Elvis had a voice that could explain the sexuality of America."

Inquiry into sex abuse at boys' homes

Power and money turn men into adulterers

b) Sex should never be used by a person simply to satisfy their own lust (sexual desires). That is a denial of all that is good and pure about sex. Misused, sex can become the most selfish of activities. Too often in sex outside marriage, the most important elements are missing.

c) Sexual intercourse is so special that, in the New Testament, it is likened to the relationship between Christ and the Church. Roman Catholics, in particular, would point out that it is very special since it is the God-given means of creating new life.

d) Sex is the most beautiful expression of a growing and life-long relationship between two people. Again, this can only take place between two people who are married to each other.

Having said this, there are some people who believe that God has called them to live 'celibate' lives. Roman Catholic priests, monks and nuns all vow that they will lead lives without entering into any kind of sexual relationship. This will be discussed further in Unit 2.7.

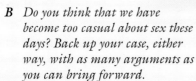

B   Do you think that we have become too casual about sex these days? Back up your case, either way, with as many arguments as you can bring forward.

WHAT DO YOU THINK?

Paul was responsible for some controversial teaching about sex and its relationship with marriage. He wrote the following:

> "To the unmarried…I say this…if they do not have self-control they should marry."
> (1.Corinthians 7.8,9)

Discuss this statement with other people in your class. What exactly do you think Paul was saying. Do you agree with him?

ANSWER IN YOUR BOOK …

1   How is sexual intercourse between human beings different to mating among animals?

2   Why do many people now argue that sex outside marriage is perfectly acceptable?

3   On what basis does the Church argue that marriage is still the proper and only place in which sexual activity should take place?

IN THE GLOSSARY …

Roman Catholic Church; Priest; Celibacy; Monk; Nun.

2.3 CONTRACEPTION

Each time two people make love without using any form of contraception, around 300,000,000 (300 million) sperm are released into the woman's body. It takes just one of these sperm to fertilise the woman's egg and conception takes place. To avoid an unwanted pregnancy, therefore, some form of effective contraception is essential.

Different terms

There are three important terms here and they each mean something slightly different:

1 *Birth-control*. When a country, such as India or China, wishes to limit its exploding population it issues guidelines to the people. Any device used to limit the number of babies born in this, or similar, situations is called 'birth control'.
2 *Family Planning*. One couple may decide that they do not want to have children. Another couple may believe that their family is large enough already and they do not want to have any more children. A third newly married couple may want to wait before they have any children and another couple may want more children but not just yet. All of them will use contraceptives as a means of 'family planning' so that they achieve the family they want.
3 *Contraception*. An unmarried couple who make love may simply want to avoid a pregnancy. If this is the case, they will use the various devices available to make sure it does not happen.

Methods of contraception

Not surprisingly, there is nothing in the Bible about contraception. Until the 1930s in Great Britain, all of the major Christian Churches were against any interference with the natural processes of nature. The great change in attitude came during the Depression of the 1930s. The link between the number of children in a family and the poverty in which they lived became very clear. Most Churches accepted that some form of 'birth prevention', as it was then called, was necessary. Since then, only the Roman Catholic Church has

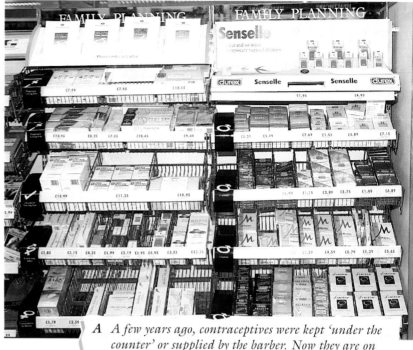

A *A few years ago, contraceptives were kept 'under the counter' or supplied by the barber. Now they are on open display. What has happened to change the attitude of the general public towards them?*

remained totally opposed to all forms of artificial birth-control.

Among the methods now available are the following:

a) *The Pill*. Over 3,000,000 women in the U.K. and 50,000,000 women worldwide now use this method. It is claimed to be 98% reliable although some women suffer side-effects from taking it.
b) *The IUD or coil*. This is placed in the woman's uterus by a doctor and left in place. It is only fitted in women who have had children and is rather controversial. It seems to work by bringing about a 'spontaneous abortion' if a fertilised egg imbeds itself in the wall of the uterus. Christians who feel strongly about abortion do not approve of the Intra Uterine Device.
c) *The cap or diaphragm*. A circular, rubber device which a woman fits over the neck of her cervix before she has sex and then leaves in place for several hours afterwards. It acts as a barrier against the sperm.

d) *The condom or sheath.* A tube of thin latex which a man fits over his erect penis before he comes into any sexual contact with the woman. The condom offers real protection against sexually transmitted diseases and AIDS as well as being an effective contraceptive.

e) *Sterilisation of the man or woman.* In the man's case the tube which carries the sperm to the penis is cut and in the woman's case the fallopian tubes which carry the egg to the uterus are cut. This is particularly unacceptable to the Catholic Church since it makes a person infertile. The Church teaches that everyone should be open to the possibility of creating new life each time they have sex.

B *What do you think a couple need to bear in mind when they are choosing which contraceptive to use?*

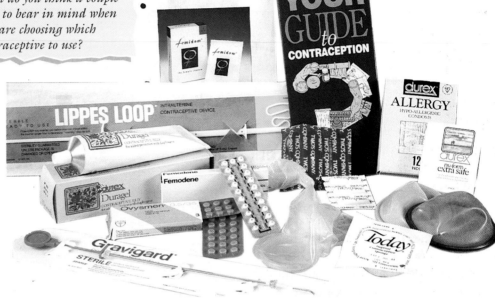

ANSWER IN YOUR BOOK ...

1 What is meant by the terms contraception, family planning and birth-control.

2 Why did most Christian Churches eventually come to accept the concept of people being able to limit the size of their families?

3 What are the main methods of birth-control?

READ AND DECIDE ...

The Roman Catholic objection to all 'unnatural' forms of birth control was stated in the document Humanae Vitae, published on July 25th, 1968. It said:

"...condemned is any action, which either before, or at the moment of, or after sexual intercourse is specifically intended to prevent procreation – whether as an end or a means...It is never lawful, even for the gravest reasons, to do evil that good may come of it..."

a) As 'natural family planning' is the only method sanctioned by the Roman Catholic Church, can you find out what it is and how it works?

b) As many Roman Catholic countries have among the fastest-growing populations in the world, can you find out what this ruling is doing to the world's population?

WHAT DO YOU THINK?

Here are two quotations. Read them and think about their implications as far as the world's population is concerned:

a) Genesis 1.28:
"God blessed them and said to them, Be fruitful and increase, fill the earth..."

b) Psalm 127.4,5:
"Like arrows in the hand of a warrior
are the sons of one's youth.
Happy is he
who has his quiver full of them; "

Do you look upon children as a blessing? Give reasons for your answer.

IN THE GLOSSARY ...

Contraception; Birth-control; Family Planning; Conception; Bible; Roman Catholic Church.

2.4 WHAT IS MARRIAGE?

Marriage is a close relationship between a man and a woman. It may take different forms but it is common in every society. The normal requirement is that both partners should be unmarried at the time of marrying (monogamy). Occasionally, however, one of them, usually the man, is allowed to have more than one partner (polygamy). Most societies recognise children born within marriage as 'legitimate'. Those born outside a married relationship are 'illegitimate' or 'bastards'. This is a particularly important point when property is passed on from parents to children.

Why get married?

There has been a steady decline in the number of marriages performed in the U.K. since the early 1970s. By 1993 the figure was around 300,000 – the lowest number of marriages for many years. This decline may be partly due to economic circumstances. Couples cannot afford to marry. It is more likely, however, to be due to a change in attitudes as 75% of couples now live together before they marry.

Of those couples who marry around 50% do so in a church or other religious building and a similar number go through a non-religious ceremony in a Registry Office. The number of those having a civil (non-religious) ceremony has increased considerably in recent years. Part of the reason for this is that the major Churches still refuse to marry people who have been divorced. It also reflects the fact that less than 10% of the population now attend church regularly.

Despite the drop in the overall number of marriages there is no real sign that marriage, as an institution, is dying out. 98% of the adult population marry at some time with over 90% of women and 80% of men marrying before they reach their 30th birthday. Even divorce does not seem to put people off marriage since 75% of divorcees re-marry within five years.

Why, then, do people marry?

1 To express their love and commitment to each other.
2 So that they can live together with the approval and support of their family and friends.
3 To gain the security of a permanent relationship that cannot be easily broken.
4 So that they can have children and bring them up in a stable environment.
5 So that their sexual drives can be channelled in an appropriate way.
6 For friendship and companionship throughout their married lives together.

A *What do you think are the main hopes and aspirations of this couple as they begin their married life together?*

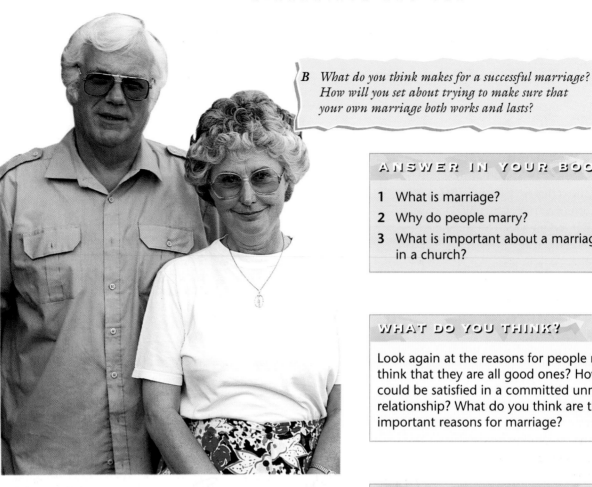

B What do you think makes for a successful marriage? How will you set about trying to make sure that your own marriage both works and lasts?

Marriage in church

A wedding in a church of any denomination combines the legal and religious elements of marriage. Although there are small variations, each wedding service emphasises the same basic ingredients:

a) That God has given us marriage for three distinct purposes:
   ❖ for two people to live together and support each other;
   ❖ for two people to enjoy a sexual relationship;
   ❖ for two people to become parents.

b) A ring is placed upon the woman's finger and often on the man's as well. The ring is a symbol of everlasting love.

c) The priest assures the couple that they have been married 'in the sight (or presence) of God.' Although friends and relations are present as 'witnesses', it is the Divine witness (God) who really matters. That is why the priest reminds them of the words in the Gospels:

> "What God has joined together let no one tear asunder."

ANSWER IN YOUR BOOK ...

1 What is marriage?

2 Why do people marry?

3 What is important about a marriage that takes place in a church?

WHAT DO YOU THINK?

Look again at the reasons for people marrying. Do you think that they are all good ones? How many of them could be satisfied in a committed unmarried relationship? What do you think are the three most important reasons for marriage?

CAN YOU EXPLAIN?

a) Can you explain just what a 'vow' is and why you think that it plays such a central role in a wedding service?

b) Can you explain why marriage appears to have lost some of its attraction in recent years?

c) Can you explain what you think society, and individuals within it, would lose if marriage was ever abolished?

d) Can you explain what you think the essential difference is between a marriage carried out in a church and one performed in a Registry Office? In which of the two locations would you feel happiest marrying in? Can you explain why?

e) If you were asked to come up with three reasons for having a church wedding service, what would you say? Can you explain your answer?

IN THE GLOSSARY ...

Heterosexual; Monogamy; Polygamy.

2.5 SEX AND MARRIAGE

When two people marry in a church they are told that they are entering into a commitment for life. This is the teaching of the whole Christian Church and explains why most Churches find it very difficult to come to terms with divorce (see Unit 2.6). Roman Catholics, in particular, argue that the marriage vows (promises) cannot be broken or the marriage dissolved.

Sex and marriage

Surveys show clearly that only about 20% of the population are virgins when they marry. Indeed, over 50% of the population have lost their virginity by the time they reach their 18th birthday. Statistics like these alarm many Christians. So does the fact that three out of every four couples now live together before they marry. Christians emphasise the unhappy consequences of so much sexual activity taking place outside marriage. In particular, they draw attention to the following:

a) The risks of unwanted pregnancies, the increasing number of abortions and the ever-growing number of one-parent families.
b) The danger of sexually-transmitted diseases and AIDS.
c) The number of marriages which break down because one, or both, people have been unfaithful.

These are problems for all societies in the modern world. In the U.S.A. some religious groups and churches have tried to correct the trend by preaching a message of 'celibacy until marriage'. This message is now an essential part of many sex education lessons in American schools.

The Bible and marriage

The Christian view of marriage and sexual relationships is based, in part, upon the teachings of the Old Testament. The ancient Hebrews believed that every girl had to be a virgin at the time of her marriage and had to remain completely faithful to her husband. Those caught committing the act of adultery were stoned to death.

Adultery is also condemned in the New Testament. The emphasis there is upon the 'oneness' of the relationship between a husband and wife. Two quotations make this clear:

1 **Mark. 10.6-8:**
"…in the beginning, at the creation, God made them male and female. That is why a man leaves his father and mother, and is united to his wife, and the two become one flesh. It follows that they are no longer two individuals: they are one flesh."
2 **1.Corinthians 7.3-4:**
"The husband must give his wife what is due to her, and equally the wife must give her husband his due. The wife cannot claim her body as her own; it is her husband's. Equally, the husband cannot claim his body as his own; it is his wife's."

A If either of these people were to be involved in a serious 'affair' what effect do you think it would have on their marriage? Make a list of the likely, and possible, effects.

B   Would you advise this couple to live together before they marry or not? Can you explain and justify your answer either way?

1   What do Christians believe when they enter into marriage?

2   What did the ancient Hebrews believe about marriage?

3   What is the emphasis in the New Testament concerning marriage?

Here are three common statements made about marriage and sex. Map out the answer that you would make to each of them. Then discuss your answers with other people in your class. Finally, write up your answers, suitably considered, into your books:

a) **Alan, 23:** "I do not think that it is possible any longer to promise to stay with the same person for ever. Perhaps the marriage vows should be renewed – say, every five years?"

b) **Anna, 27:** "I do not think it matters how many sexual relationships you have before you marry. In fact, it is probably better to be sexually experienced before you marry. That way, you are less likely to make mistakes."

c) **Alan, 31:** " I do not think that the odd affair after marriage is any great problem. Obviously, affairs can break a marriage but they do not need to. A little give and take is all that is needed."

The Bible is talking here about sexual responsibility. In its view such responsibility can be described in the following ways:

a) The proper place for sexual activity is within the discipline of marriage.

2   Within marriage the husband and wife have sexual responsibilities towards each other which they must both fulfil.

3   Marriage is a sexually exclusive relationship. There can be no room for extra-marital affairs in a Christian marriage.

Do you think that this teaching is realistic in the modern age?

Roman Catholic Church; Vows; Virgin; Abortion; Sexually Transmitted Diseases; AIDS; Celibacy; Old Testament; Hebrews; New Testament.

2.6 DIVORCE

An increasing number of marriages do not live up to the expectations of one, or both, partners involved. In the U.K. around 45% of all marriages now end in divorce. This amounts to the break-up of some 180,000 relationships each year. In most of these cases, the adults suffer great stress. However, the main losers are almost always the children involved.

How, though, did this state of affairs come about?

Divorce and the law

Before 1857 divorce was a long and very expensive business. The following then happened:

a) In 1857 the Matrimonial Causes Act came into existence. This made the divorce procedure easier and less expensive. For the first time both men and women could obtain a divorce. However, it remained much easier for men for the following reasons:
   ❖ a woman had to demonstrate that her husband had committed adultery and also some other 'matrimonial offence', such as desertion or cruelty;
   ❖ a man only had to prove that his wife had committed adultery.

b) In 1923 another Act put men and women on exactly the same footing.

c) Leglislation in 1937 extended the grounds for divorce to include desertion, cruelty and insanity.

d) The Divorce Reform Act of 1969 changed the whole emphasis of the law. People could now obtain a divorce if they could show that their marriage:

   "…had irretrievably broken down…"

Adultery, cruelty and desertion could be used to demonstrate this. For the first time, a divorce could be obtained if only one person wanted it although a five-year separation period was necessary.

The aftermath

The number of divorces increased dramatically as a result of this legislation. Among the consequences of making divorce easier many people would list the following:

1 There are now over 1,200,000 single-parent families in the U.K. The vast majority of these have come about as the result of divorce.

2 75% of all divorcing couples have children under the age of 16. There are now 1,250,000 such children in the U.K. and this number is growing all the time.

A Do you think that people could be trained for marriage, so cutting down on the number of divorces?

How children are damaged by divorce

Camilla parts from husband

Royal divorce will go ahead, says courtier

Breakdown rates
Divorce help

Couples get period to reflect on divorce

£50m divorce deal

Mediation could save marriages, claims Mackay

Law and church welcome end to quickie divorces

C of E reviews wedding ban on divorcees

Cabinet will end 'quickie' divorces

Divorced wives may get half of pension money

divorcees

House blown up in divorce battle

divorce

Mackay seeks end to 'quickie' divorces

Three runaway sisters try to mend their parents' broken marriage

3 Many couples no longer see marriage as a full-time commitment. Instead of working hard at their marriages, when problems arise they take the easy way out.

4 Easy divorce devalues marriage at a time when marriage is more important than ever in our society.

Christians and divorce

Jesus had as much to say about divorce as almost any other issue. Unfortunately, the meaning of his comments, recorded in the Gospels, are not absolutely clear. You will discover this for yourself if you look at them closely. As a result, the different Churches

B   What do you think are the main problems likely to be caused by two people divorcing?

have come to their own rather different conclusions about divorce. These attitudes fall into three groups:

a) The Roman Catholic Church will not accept or recognise divorce in any way.

b) The Church of England will accept divorce but will not officially re-marry divorced people.

c) The Protestant Free Churches allow divorced people to re-marry in church although individual ministers can refuse to do so if it conflicts with their own personal beliefs.

ANSWER IN YOUR BOOK ...

1 Outline the changes in the law about divorce which have taken place since 1857.

2 What changes were introduced by the Divorce Reform Act of 1967?

3 What are some of the consequences of divorce for many families?

DISCUSS AMONG YOURSELVES ...

Malcolm Wickes, the former Director of the Family Policy Studies Centre, had this to say:

"The causes of divorce spring from fundamental social, economic and psychological developments that are occurring worldwide."

Discuss among yourselves just what you think he meant. Come up with examples of the following pressures which might account for the increase in the number of divorces:

❖ Social

❖ Economic

❖ Psychological

READ AND DECIDE ...

Here are some passages for you to read which outline the teaching of the New Testament about divorce.

a) Matthew 19.3-9

b) Mark 10.11,12

c) I.Corinthians 7.10,11,27

a) On what basis from the Old Testament did Jesus insist that when two people marry they become one flesh? What conclusion did he draw from this?

b) Why did Jesus say that Moses, the great Jewish leader, allowed divorce? What exception did Jesus seem to make to his own ban on divorce?

c) What comment of Jesus does Mark record regarding those who divorce and then marry someone else?

d) What does Paul tell those people who have divorced?

IN THE GLOSSARY ...

Adultery.

2.7 CELIBACY, CHASTITY AND VIRGINITY

We cannot be sure but it seems likely that there was a strong tradition of celibacy (an unmarried state, usually maintained for religious reasons) in the early Christian Church. St Paul was certainly unmarried. He wrote to the Christians in Corinth:

> "I should like everyone to be as I myself am (unmarried)... (1.Corinthians 7.7)

For centuries many Christians remained unmarried, especially those living as hermits or monks, but the decision always remained a voluntary one. Then, in 1139, the Catholic Church decreed that all of its priests should be celibate. It was thought that the unmarried priest could devote himself totally to God in a way that the married man could not. The Catholic Church remains the only denomination in which celibacy is still required for its priests. Although there are many voices within the Catholic Church demanding a change the present Pope, John Paul II, has declared that the rule will remain in operation. As a consequence, thousands of priests have left the Catholic Church in recent years in order to marry.

Virginity

A 'virgin' is someone, male or female, who has never had sexual intercourse. In the U.K. the law implies that everyone should remain a virgin until they reach the age of 16, since that is when sexual intercourse becomes legal. However, statistics indicate that 25% of young people lose their virginity before their 16th birthday and that only 25% are virgins by the time they are 18.

Previous generations have prized virginity more highly than we seem to do today. There were several reasons for this:

a) In the time before contraception was readily available, abstention from sexual contact and intercourse was the only safeguard against pregnancy.

b) A line was drawn between the sexual activity of men and women. While it was acceptable for men to 'sow their wild oats', women were expected to be virgins when they married. It was, of course, totally hypocritical but that is the way that people thought.

c) There was an unspoken fear of contracting sexually transmitted diseases. This was, of course, well before the time of AIDS but gonorrhoea and syphilis were largely untreatable.

There are still, of course, many young people who believe that it is important to remain virgins until they marry. The teaching of almost all the Christian Churches is that sexual relationships outside marriage are sinful. Many Christians highlight the sad consequences of the so-called 'sexual revolution' of the 1960s and argue that sexual abstinence until marriage is in everyone's best interests.

Chastity

Chastity means that an individual makes the decision to live a life free from sexual relations. He or she might make such a decision for purely personal reasons. For instance, they may have a very low sex drive, they may have

A *There is a serious lack of priests entering the Catholic priesthood. Do you think that the requirement of celibacy is likely to be one of the reasons for this?*

lost interest in sex or there may be medical reasons why sexual activity is not possible or desirable. Many people who have HIV, for example, live chaste lives because they do not want to risk passing the virus on to someone else. That is a very responsible decision for them to take.

There may be other reasons why a person decides to be chaste. St Paul suggests that a Christian couple might abstain from sexual intercourse for a time to devote themselves to prayer (1.Corinthians 7.5). In this case, however, normal sexual relations are resumed after a time. If a couple wish to follow the teaching of the Roman Catholic Church on birth-control, they will need to be chaste for a certain period every month. 'Chastity' is one of the three vows, together with poverty and obedience, which is demanded of everyone, male and female, who wish to enter a monastery or a convent.

B Why do you think that Pope John Paul II has maintained such strong support for celibacy among the Roman Catholic clergy?

ANSWER IN YOUR BOOK ...

1 What did Paul have to say about the unmarried, celibate state?

2 Why might an individual or a married couple choose to live a temporary, or permanently, chaste life?

3 Why was virginity prized more highly in the past than it generally is today?

COMPLETE A CHART ...

The question of priestly celibacy in the Roman Catholic Church is likely to become a very heated topic in the coming years. Draw up a table like the one below in your books and try to produce five arguments in favour of priestly celibacy and five against.

PRIESTLY CELIBACY

What is priestly celibacy? ....
....

	ARGUMENTS FOR	ARGUMENTS AGAINST
1		
2		
3		
4		
5		

IN YOUR OWN WORDS ...

In your own words, describe the meaning of each of the following:

a) Celibacy

b) Chastity

c) Virginity

IN THE GLOSSARY ...

Celibacy; Paul; Hermit; Monk; Roman Catholic Church; Priest; Chastity; Virgin.

2.8 HOMOSEXUALITY

Homosexuality (from the Latin word 'homo' meaning 'same') describes sexual relationships between people of the same sex, whether male or female. Although homosexuality dates back at least to the ancient Greeks, we have only recently begun to understand it. For a very long time it was assumed that homosexuals were simply heterosexuals who had, for some reason, chosen to indulge in same-sex relationships. In coining the word 'homosexual' in 1869 the obscure Hungarian doctor, Karoly Benkert, was pointing out that homosexuals were a separate group of people. What is more, they had different sexual attitudes and interests to heterosexuals.

Concerning names

A Do you think that society finds it any easier to accept lesbianism than homosexuality?

The word 'lesbian' was brought into use in the 19th century to describe female homosexuals. The word was taken from the Greek island of Lesbos where, in the 7th century BCE, the Greek poetess Sappho gathered an all-female community around herself.

In recent years the male homosexual community has preferred to call itself 'gay' rather than homosexual. This is to counter the idea that a homosexual is a miserable, depressed individual.

Worldwide, there are millions of men and women who have adopted a gay lifestyle. Like heterosexuals, homosexuals are drawn from every walk of life: rich and poor; educated and illiterate; powerful and powerless and the happy and near-suicidal.

Homosexuals are found in all nations, races, social classes and religious groups. They live in every town, city and village. They are part of the fabric of our society.

No one knows just how many homosexuals there are. It is thought that for every homosexual who 'comes out' (makes their homosexuality known) at least ten continue to keep it a secret. It has been assumed for some time that about one in ten of the population is gay. If so, this would mean that in Great Britain alone 1,900,000 men and 600,000 women are homosexual. Recent studies, however, suggest that this figure may be too high.

Why are people homosexual?

No one is sure. Theories, though, suggest the following:

1 *People are born homosexual.* It is part of their genetic make-up and there is nothing they can do about it, even if they wanted to.
2 *Family background or family circumstances affect a person's sexual orientation.* It has been suggested, for instance, that boys who have unnaturally strong links with their mothers, and weak relationships with their fathers, are more likely to develop homosexual tendencies.
3 *Everyone has the potential to be either homosexual or heterosexual.* How we turn out depends on influences in our childhood and on our early sexual experiences.

Homosexuality and the law

Until 1967 it was illegal for a man to be a practising homosexual in the U.K. In that year, homosexual relationships were made legal as long as the following conditions were satisfied:

a) They were conducted between consenting adults aged 21 or over. In 1994 this age limit was reduced to 18.

b) They were conducted in private.

Most of the Christian Churches draw a distinction between homosexual feelings and homosexual acts. They accept that love is to be welcomed in every situation, no matter what the sex of the people concerned. Taking its lead from the Bible, however, it condemns homosexual acts as being against the will of God. The Roman Catholic Church calls such acts 'unnatural' while the Church of England finds them unacceptable, especially for the clergy.

Lesbian militants target gay men

Sacked servicemen fight to end military ban on homosexuals

Bishop forced to speak out by gay group

My boy was lured away by gays and youth workers

Gay demonstration names 10 bishops

Forces ban on gays must go

Gay misery of military marching orders

Ban on gay sex stays, says Carey

India gays hide from hostile public

Campaign for gay clergy raises fears

Churchmen angered by naming of 'gay' bishops

Carey stays firm on gay clergy

Reconciling religion and homosexuality

Osborne's ex-wife denies writer was homosexual

Actor's gay partner

Churchgoers' uncertain welcome to gay clergy

Lesbian can challenge MoD

B Can you find out what homophobia is? Do these headlines suggest that we live in a homophobic society? If so, can you suggest any reasons for this?

ANSWER IN YOUR BOOK ...

1 What is homosexuality?

2 What do the terms 'homosexual' and 'lesbian' mean?

3 What explanations have been put forward to explain why some people adopt a homosexual lifestyle and others do not?

WRITE AN ESSAY ...

Homosexual activity is not new. It was also practiced in Biblical times as the following references make clear. Read them carefully:

❖ Genesis 19
❖ Leviticus 18.22
❖ I.Corinthians 6.9-10

Make your own notes on these verses and then write an essay entitled 'The Bible and Homosexuality'.

Make sure you explain the terms that you use at the beginning of the essay.

FIND OUT AND NOTE ...

Try to find out what a 'phobia' is. How many different kinds of phobia can you list? What do you think 'homophobia' is? Also, try to find out the following:

a) How it affects people?

b) What it can lead people to do?

c) Why it is so dangerous?

Why do you think that homosexuality arouses such strong feelings in people?

WHAT DO YOU THINK?

Almost all Christian Churches draw a sharp distinction between homosexual feelings and homosexual acts.

a) Why do you think they do this?

b) Why do you think that they find one acceptable but not the other?

c) Do you think that it is fair to expect some men and women to have strong homosexual feelings but to deny them the right to express those feelings physically?

IN THE GLOSSARY ...

Homosexual; Lesbianism.

35

Until the 7th century BCE people were able to obtain what they wanted by bartering or payment in kind. For example, if you wanted a new cooking pot you might ask the village potter to make it for you in return for some eggs or vegetables which you could provide. A few societies still operate in this way but bartering only really works within the small confines of a village.

People gradually began to exchange goods in return for small pieces of metal of standard weight and shape and so coins were born. To begin with, these coins had real value in themselves but their value soon became symbolic rather than actual. This has remained the case ever since. In our society banknotes, cheques, credit cards and postal orders do not have any actual worth. It is what they represent that matters. Their value lies in the wealth and standing of the bank or institution which issues them.

Sharing the wealth

Without any question, money is one of the main motivations behind people working. As everyone knows, we all need money to survive. Without it, life can be very miserable. Even in today's world millions of people still starve to death. Each winter many old people suffer from

hypothermia because they cannot afford to heat their homes adequately. Over 2,000,000 people in the U.K. alone cannot find work and have to manage on very basic State benefits. We seem to live in a society which behaves as if material benefits are all that matter. Writing to Timothy, Paul was moved to comment that:

"The love of money is the root of all evil." (1.Timothy 6.10)

Paul was merely underlining the teaching that Jesus had already given. Confronted by poverty all around, Jesus constantly emphasised the dangers that wealth brought. He even stated that such wealth could easily prevent a man from entering God's kingdom – Mark 10.17-21 ; Luke 18.25. For many of his listeners this was one of the toughest things that Jesus ever said. Why, though, do you think he saw that wealth could prevent many people from entering His kingdom?

Debt

Early in 1989 the Citizen's Advice Bureau revealed that it now advises more people in the U.K. about

A We are told that we will soon live in a society in which people will not need to carry money around with them. Do you think that this will be good thing or do you foresee it creating some real problems? If so, what do you think the problems might be?

B 'Plastic' money has become an essential part of modern life. Do you see any dangers in this?

1 What is bartering?

2 Why do you think that Jesus and Paul insisted that material wealth was not the only thing that mattered in life?

3 Why do many people get themselves into debt?

WHAT DO YOU THINK?

The words of Paul to Timothy are often misquoted. Read them again carefully.
 "The love of money is the root of all evil"
 (1.Timothy 6.10)

a) People often think that Paul was insisting that money is the root of all evil. What do you think is the difference between insisting that money is the root of all evil and stating that it is the love of money which is at the root of all our problems?

b) Do you think that Paul was right to insist that the 'love of money' is the root of all evil? Which international, social and personal problems can you think of which are caused mainly by greed and the love of money?

c) Why do you think that the love of money has the power to cause so much unhappiness and so many problems?

WRITE AN ESSAY ...

The Bible has quite a lot to say about money, material wealth and the dangers of both. Read for yourself and make notes:

a) Psalm 50.12
b) Ecclesiastes 5.19
c) Luke 12.15
d) 2.Corinthians 9.7-8
e) Mark 10.17-21
f) Matthew 6.24
g) Luke 18.25

Now write an essay with the title:
'The Bible, wealth and money'.

IN THE GLOSSARY ...

Bartering; Paul; Redundancy.

debt than about any other problem. It appears that the average British family is now in debt to six different companies and carries three credit cards. Why do people get themselves into debt?

a) They are trying to manage on a very low income.
b) They have difficulty in managing their money (they spend more than they earn).
c) They are suddenly overwhelmed by family problems such as the main bread-winner being made redundant.
d) They have found it too easy to obtain credit – "Buy now, pay later."

Why do you think that debt is such a serious social problem? What kind of problems might it lead to?

3.2 WHY WORK?

In the U.K. there are some 26,000,000 (26 million) adults in paid employment. Most of them work in one of three different areas:

1 *Primary industries.* These are industries which exploit our natural resources such as mining, agriculture and fishing. The number of jobs in these industries has declined dramatically in recent years.
2 *Secondary or manufacturing industries.* Such industries include car production, electronics and chemicals.
3 *Tertiary or service industries.* These industries provide services such as banking, shops, estate agents and tourist facilities. The number of people working in these industries has gone up dramatically since the 2nd World War but is now declining.

There is another factor which needs to be considered. In the opening sentence we spoke of those people in 'paid employment'. The figures quoted do not include the millions of people who work long, hard hours without being paid. Parents of small children, housewives and those who care for elderly and sick relatives all 'work' but are not included in the numbers of those 'employed'.

Why work?

There are several reasons why people work:

a) *To satisfy basic needs.* These include food, clothing and shelter. In most Western countries people in work earn enough money to meet these needs. Indeed, they work not only to meet their 'needs' but to satisfy their 'wants' as well. The desire for more material security – a bigger house or car, more exotic holidays, etc – make many people work harder and longer hours. Ironically, if they are not careful, they find that they no longer have the time to enjoy the fruits of their wealth. All of us know of such 'workaholics'. In most of the developing world, however, this is far from the case. Wages can barely meet the minimum needs of the family. Everyone is involved in the never-ending struggle to stay alive. The family will grow just enough to meet their own needs but have little left over to sell. 'Subsistence farming' manages to keep most families alive but only just.

> **A** *If many children did not look after their sick and elderly relatives, then society would have to do so. Do you think these 'carers' should be paid for what they do?*

B *Most people who suddenly become unemployed say that they miss the social aspect of their old job almost as much as the money. Why do you think that working with others is so important for most people?*

b) *To achieve self-respect and personal satisfaction.* Work, as we have already said, is an essential part of being human. Most peoples' identity and self-worth is closely linked to their occupation. This is why so many people go through an 'identity crisis' if they lose their job and become unemployed.

c) *To find a sense of achievement and fulfillment.* For many, work only represents boredom and drudgery. For others, however, it brings a sense of satisfaction and achievement. As we shall see in Unit 3.3, Christians believe that any job, no matter how mundane, should be done as well as possible – to the glory of God.

d) *For contact with other people.* This is an aspect of work that is often forgotten yet most people need to interact with their colleagues at work in the atmosphere of a busy working environment. For example, some parents of small children return to work part-time for the stimulus of adult company.

e) *To maintain and control the environment.* Many basic occupations such as fishing and farming, for example, bring people into contact with the world around them. This involvement with the natural world is stressed in the book of Genesis: "God blessed them and said to them, Be fruitful and increase, fill the earth and subdue it, have dominion over…" (Genesis 1.28)

The natural environment needs the graft of hard work. Human beings need to work. Society benefits from having a satisfied and fulfilled work-force.

IN YOUR OWN WORDS …

a) Do you think that people find it difficult to distinguish between a 'need' and a 'want'? How would you distinguish between the two?

b) What is the Christian ideal of work? Do you think it is possible to live up to this ideal?

c) Many unemployed people speak of their feelings of isolation. What do you think they mean by this?

d) What would happen if people did not work to control the environment?

e) Why do you think that work is important to so many people?

ANSWER IN YOUR BOOK …

1 What is the difference between primary, secondary and tertiary industries?

2 Who are the 'carers' in our society?

3 Why do people work?

WRITE AN ESSAY …

Write an essay of about 500 words on the topic:
  'Why do people need to work?'

Before you begin to write, try to interview some working people to find out just what it is that they get out of work.

3.3 VOCATION

When Christians talk about work you will often hear them using the word 'vocation'. It comes from the Latin word meaning 'to be called'. In Christian circles it is often used in more than one way:

1 It can refer to a special 'calling' from God to do a specifically religious job of work. To take three examples:
   ❖ Missionaries who leave their home country to serve God elsewhere usually refer to their 'calling' or vocation.
   ❖ Roman Catholic men who feel 'called' to the priesthood then have that calling 'tested' through undergoing six years of training.
   ❖ Some Roman Catholics and Anglicans may feel that they have been called to the 'religious life' to live as monks or nuns.

Traditionally, the Roman Catholic Church has taught that such a 'religious calling' is higher than any other but the Second Vatican Council firmly rejected this view. It emphasised that every Christian 'calling', whether to a religious vocation or not, is equally important in the sight of God.

B *What does it mean to call every job of work a 'vocation'?*

A *What do you think this doctor gains from his job? Would you describe what he is doing as a 'calling'?*

2 Some people believe that they have been called by God into a certain job. These jobs require particular personal characteristics such as being a doctor, a nurse or a teacher. You will often hear these occupations being referred to as the 'caring professions' since they demand a high level of personal self-sacrifice and commitment. They make heavy demands on the people involved and are not the best-paid occupations in society. In recent years there have been bitter disputes and strikes involving members of the 'caring professions', demanding better rates of pay and working conditions. This included junior hospital doctors, for example, who traditionally had been expected to work over 80 hours a week including shifts of 48 hours! Society has clearly taken them for granted for a very long time.

3 Martin Luther, the Protestant Reformer, introduced another element into our understanding of 'vocation'. His idea has become known as the 'Protestant Work Ethic'. It teaches that everyone has a vocation from God to serve him just where they are. Their responsibility is to do their job to

C *This montage shows a traditional approach to work. Do you think that in the future the nature of work in the U.K. and overseas will change drastically?*

A Christian approach to work

The Bible insists that all people should serve God by doing their work to the glory of God. Of course, if people are to look on their work as a vocation and commit themselves to it wholeheartedly, two conditions must be met by others in society:

the very best of their ability. All Christians have this vocation but what difference do you think it might actually make in the workplace?

a) Society as a whole must appreciate what they are doing and pay them accordingly. So often in the past we have taken those in the 'caring professions' for granted and treated them shabbily. We have then complained bitterly when they have protested. Jesus taught that 'a labourer is worthy of his hire'.

b) Both employers and employees must accept that they have certain responsibilities towards each other. Neither must take advantage of the other.

ANSWER IN YOUR BOOK ...

1 What is a vocation?
2 How did Martin Luther provide a new and much wider understanding of the meaning of a vocation?
3 What should be the biblical principle underlying the Christian approach to all work?

READ AND DECIDE ...

Here are two quotations from the Bible. Read them carefully and then try to work out just what their full application in the work-place, and elsewhere, might mean.

a) **Mark 10.43-45:**
"(Jesus said), You know that among the Gentiles the recognized rulers lord it over their subjects, and the great make their authority felt. It shall not be so with you; among you, whoever wants to be great must be your servant, and whoever wants to be first must be the slave of all. For the Son of Man (Jesus) did not come to be served but to serve, and to give his life as ransom for many."

b) **Colossians 3.23:**
"Whatever you are doing, put your whole heart into it, as if you were doing it for the Lord and not for men."

WHAT DO YOU THINK?

a) Do you think that society takes for granted the work that is being done by people in the 'caring professions'. If they feel that they are being taken for granted do you think that people in such professions should, in the last resort, go on strike?

b) What responsibilities do you think employers and employees have towards each other?

c) Do you think that it is possible to look on any job, whatever it is, as a vocation (a calling from God). If so, what practical difference do you think this might make to how a person does a job?

IN THE GLOSSARY ...

Missionary; Priesthood, Monk; Nun; Second Vatican Council.

3.4 UNEMPLOYMENT

It is not easy to decide just how many people are out of work at any given time. For most of the early 1990s the 'official' figure of unemployed in the U.K. was well over the 2,000,000 mark, a figure that began to decline early in 1993. This figure, however, does not tell us the true situation. The following also has to be taken into consideration:

a) Only those people who receive State benefits and are registered as unemployed are included in the figures.

b) Married women, who cannot claim benefit if their husbands are employed, are excluded. Furthermore, if their husband is also unemployed then the benefit is paid out in his name.

c) The figure excludes thousands of young people on training schemes, all unemployed men over the age of 60 and the many 'down and outs' and 'travellers' in society.

What causes unemployment?

Most countries today have a severe unemployment problem. The current situation in the U.K. has mainly been caused by the following:

1 A decline in manufacturing industries in the face of intense competition from overseas. To take just one example. Thousands of miners have lost their jobs in recent years and many pits have closed. The main reason for this? Power-stations and other heavy users of coal can buy more cheaply from Poland and other European countries.

2 An increase in mechanisation and automation. Inevitably the use of computers and other mechanised forms of running businesses has led to many people losing their jobs. This has happened particularly in such service industries as banking and insurance.

3 A growth in the number of people seeking work, especially the number of women seeking to return to paid employment. The 'working mother' is much more common now than she used to be.

B Which people do you think are most at a disadvantage in today's job market?

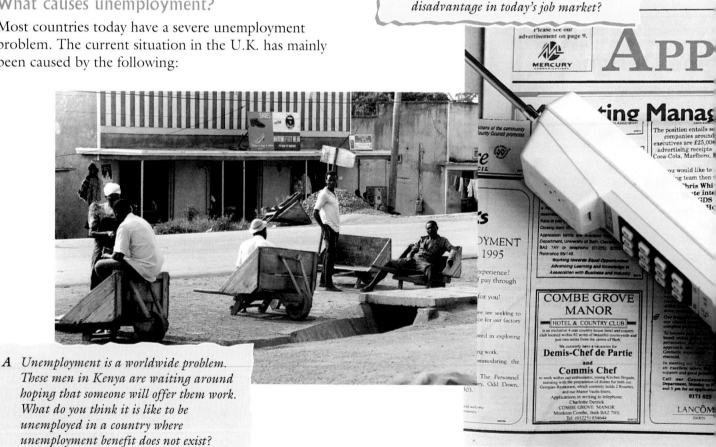

A Unemployment is a worldwide problem. These men in Kenya are waiting around hoping that someone will offer them work. What do you think it is like to be unemployed in a country where unemployment benefit does not exist?

The problem of unemployment

Can anything be done to tackle unemployment? Politicians and economists disagree about the roots and the answers to the problem. While the Conservative Party in the U.K. is generally reluctant to interfere in the jobs market, the Labour Party believes that direct intervention to create new jobs is essential. Whatever policy is adopted, however, the social and personal consequences of long-term unemployment are immense:

a) Low morale, depression, poor self-esteem and even suicide.

b) Tension within families leading to a break-down in family life.

c) An increase in drug-taking and alcohol abuse.

d) An increase in criminal behaviour and typical inner-city problems like vandalism, violence and even rioting.

e) Racial abuse and attacks.

The Church supports any measures which are designed to help the unemployed. With its churches in the inner-city areas where social problems stemming from unemployment are at their most acute, the Church is uniquely placed to understand the problem. In many places it:

❖ runs counselling and training centres to help the unemployed find work;

❖ provides food and clothing for those without any form of income;

❖ sets up schemes to help people use their enforced leisure time constructively;

❖ runs 'job clubs' to encourage and help the unemployed to find work.

ANSWER IN YOUR BOOK ...

1 Why is it very difficult to know just how many people are really unemployed at any given time?

2 Why is there a high level of unemployment in the U.K. and elsewhere?

3 What social and personal problems are often caused by unemployment?

READ AND DECIDE ...

There are several comments in the Bible about work. Look each one of them up and then answer the questions which follow:

a) **Proverbs 26.15**
Do you agree with this comment? Are some people too lazy to even put food in their own mouths, let alone anyone else's?

b) **Proverbs 26.15**
What do you think an employer should look for in someone that he or she is going to give work to?

c) **Ecclesiastes 3.13**
Is the opposite of this comment true – that we should not eat or drink unless we have worked for it?

d) **2.Thessalonians 3.6-13**
Should those people who refuse to work be barred from receiving food? What does Paul suggest that those who do not work end up doing? Do you agree?

IN THE GLOSSARY ...

Automation.

3.5 LEISURE

The United Nations Declaration on Human Rights makes the following statement:

> "Everyone has the right to rest and leisure, including reasonable working hours and holidays with pay." (Article 24)

This statement is merely following the standard first laid down in the Old Testament. From the very beginning of their history the Jews maintained that their Sabbath Day had been ordained by God as a day on which all work stopped. By following this tradition the Jews were following God's example. After spending six days in creating the world God rested from his work (Exodus 20.8,11).

Human beings need a balance of 'rest, work and play' to lead healthy and whole lives. Too much of one element and life is out of balance. The person, for instance, who works all the time (a workaholic) will end up suffering from stress and anxiety. The person who 'rests' all the time, however, is not finding the stimulation and enjoyment that work can provide.

A balanced combination of work and leisure is in the best interests of everybody.

What, though, is leisure? It can be defined in the following way:

> "The time that one has at one's own disposal."

How we spend it depends on a whole range of factors such as the money that we have to spend, the local facilities that have been provided, our age and our state of health, etc. Then, of course, our personal interests also play a crucial part in how we choose to spend our leisure time.

The 'Ages' of Leisure

While our leisure interests and activities change as we get older, it seems that most of us pass through five distinct 'ages' of leisure:

a) *The Childhood/teenage phase*. This time is mainly spent playing with our friends, taking part in sporting activities, computer activities or watching T.V. At the end of this 'age' going out, going shopping and socialising are high on the list of priorities.

b) *Early Married Life (twenties and early thirties)*. Leisure activities centre around a new home; having children; DIY; indoor hobbies, etc. Opportunities to go out are limited and so highly valued.

c) *Early Middle Age (mid thirties to around the age of fifty)*. There is now more freedom with the children growing up. More time is spent out with friends, eating out, church and other small group activities, foreign holidays, etc.

d) *Late Middle Age (between the ages of fifty and sixty-five)*. Eating out and mild physical activity such as golf and holidays are popular at this time.

e) *Old Age (sixty-five onwards)*. Knitting, gardening, walking, visiting a social club, playing with grandchildren, etc.

A *Children spend a great deal of their time being together. Why do you think this is a very important part of growing up?*

B   Do you think that it matters how people spend their leisure time?

Most people today have far more leisure time than their counterparts did a century ago. The average working week is around 37½ hours compared with double that at the end of the last century. Statistics like these, however, can be very misleading. Mothers with young children or people caring for the elderly or disabled have little leisure time. Moreover, the whole idea of leisure is meaningless to many people living in the world's developing countries who have to work through all the hours of daylight simply to survive.

A word of caution. Unlimited leisure time may sound to some like a dream come true, but for many people it is more like a nightmare. For the unemployed, the retired or those unable to work, too much leisure time can lead to boredom, frustration and depression. To make matters worse such people may have little or no money to spend on leisure activities. Boredom and 'enforced leisure' are often blamed, with good reason, for much vandalism and petty crime.

READ AND DECIDE ...

We read the following words in the Jewish Scriptures:
"Remember to keep the Sabbath Day holy. You have six days to labour and do all your work; but the seventh day is a sabbath of the Lord your God ... for in six days the Lord made the heavens and the earth, the sea, and all that is in them, and on the seventh day he rested. Therefore the Lord blessed the sabbath day and declared it holy." (Exodus 8,11)

a) Can you find out what the word 'sabbath' meant?

b) Can you find out what the link is between the Jewish sabbath day and the Christian adoption of Sunday as a holy day.

c) What do these verses suggest about the need for a sabbath day of rest?

d) In the U.K., Sunday has been turned into a day which is much like any other in the week. What do you think have been the advantages and disadvantages of doing this?

ANSWER IN YOUR BOOK ...

1 What is leisure?

2 Why is it misleading to speak of all people now having more leisure time on their hands?

3 What are the different 'ages of leisure'?

IN THE GLOSSARY ...

United Nations; Old Testament; Sabbath Day.

3.6 THE DEPRIVED

Poverty is a worldwide problem, not just a condition which is only found overseas. There is much 'relative poverty' in the U.K. By this we mean that while the 'poor' in the U.K. are 'wealthy' compared with the 'poor' overseas, they are poor compared with other people in the U.K. Poverty is, in fact, so widespread in the U.K. that people have begun to talk of there being 'two nations' – the 'haves' and the 'have-nots'.

The Poverty Line

Many countries have a minimum wage with social security benefits making sure that those people out of work or on very low wages do not fall beneath that level. In the U.K. there is not such a minimum wage although many people believe that it is essential to have one if poverty is ever going to be eradicated. Instead, there is a level of poverty from which many thousands of people have little or no hope of escaping. Even people in full-time employment can find themselves living in poverty.

Such poverty is mainly, although not exclusively, found in inner city areas. It may be caused by one or several factors:

1 *Poor housing.* We will be looking at this problem separately in Unit 3.7. Here we simply note that while poor housing is very unpleasant in itself it can lead to a whole variety of other social problems such as bad health, under-achievement at school, absenteeism from work, crime, vandalism, etc.

2 *Unemployment.* While at any given time between 2,000,000 and 3,000,000 people are likely to be unemployed in the U.K., there is a core number of some 750,000 who are considered to be unemployable. These people are drawn from the poorest in society. As far as social security is concerned, the State pays the bare minimum which is considered to be necessary to survive. People who exist solely on State benefits are among the poorest and most needy.

3 *Poor wages.* There is a vicious cycle of poverty. Some people earn very low wages and so are able to claim various State benefits and allowances. As soon as their wages increase, their State benefits decrease. Even if they are able to work more overtime they

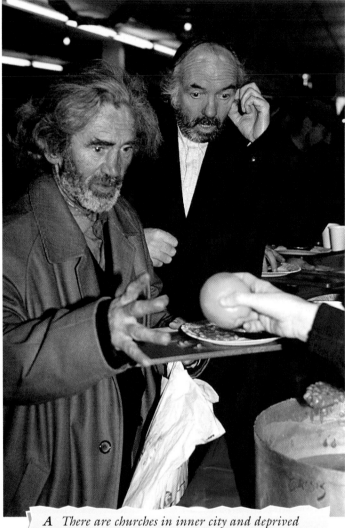

A *There are churches in inner city and deprived areas. What responsibility do you think they have to help the poor? What do you think they should actually be doing?*

find themselves hardly better off. They are caught in the so-called 'poverty trap'.

The Church and the poor

For a long time various Churches have been deeply involved in helping the poor and needy both at home and overseas. The Salvation Army, for example, is world famous in this respect. It runs night shelters, refuge centres, drop-in centres and soup runs, etc to help those who cannot help themselves. The Church of

England has had its Church Urban Fund for several years and this channels money from the wealthier churches and areas to those where poverty is most acute. At the same time there is always more that can be done. Here are some suggestions:

a) The Church is a very powerful pressure group. It should pressurise government to work harder to provide for needy people. Voluntary agencies cannot solve the problem of poverty on their own.

b) Many of the country's poorest people are black or white working class. Most of them see the Church as white and middle class. The Church must draw in more people from these backgrounds and make it possible for them to serve others through the Church.

c) The links between the churches in the wealthier areas and those in deprived parts should be greatly strengthened.

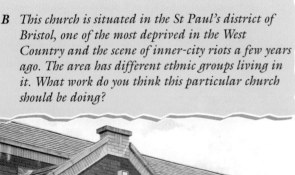

B *This church is situated in the St Paul's district of Bristol, one of the most deprived in the West Country and the scene of inner-city riots a few years ago. The area has different ethnic groups living in it. What work do you think this particular church should be doing?*

ANSWER IN YOUR BOOK ...

1 How would you describe an 'inner city' area and why do you think these areas are particularly prone to poverty?

2 What is 'Social Security' and how does it contribute to poverty?

3 What are the churches already doing to help alleviate poverty and what else might they do in the future?

WHAT DO YOU THINK?

What do you think we mean when we speak of the following:

a) The poverty line

b) The poverty trap

c) A minimum wage

d) The vicious circle of poverty

e) Relative poverty

f) Two nations

IN THE GLOSSARY ...

Third World.

3.7 HOMELESSNESS

Occasionally, the conscience of the whole country is stirred by a programme on television. This happened in the U.K. back in 1966 when the showing of the film 'Cathy Come Home' highlighted the plight of homeless people in general, and one homeless family in particular. As a result of the many gifts sent in to the Press Shelter, the National Campaign for the Homeless was set up.

Homelessness

The U.K. has a homelessness problem. It has always had this problem but the available statistics make it clear that the situation is worsening. Consider just two aspects of the overall homelessness problem:

a) The exact number of young homeless (aged 21 and under) is not easy to determine but it is thought to be between 175,000 and 200,000. Three groups of people, in particular, are heavily represented in this total:
   ❖ those who have literally nowhere to live and sleep rough on pavements, in parks, etc;
   ❖ those who live in overcrowded squats, in guest houses or in totally unsuitable accommodation;
   ❖ those who live, spasmodically or regularly, in hostel accommodation.

b) 13% of occupied housing units in the U.K. are unsatisfactory. Some 7½% are dangerous to the health and well-being of their occupants through dampness, insect infestation, etc. A further 5% lack one of the basic amenities that most of us take for granted – an inside toilet, a bath or a suitable place to cook. In all, we are talking about 2,500,000 houses, flats and maisonettes.

A What would you say were the absolutely basic housing conditions needed for human dignity to be maintained?

Bad housing is linked with a whole range of social concerns including poor health, low educational standards, the breakdown of family life, marital strife, violence and crime. It is very difficult to see how anything can be done about these crippling conditions until the housing problem is tackled.

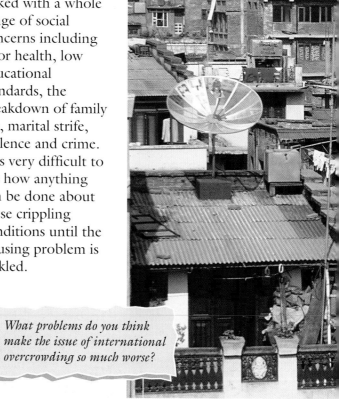

B What problems do you think make the issue of international overcrowding so much worse?

48

Shelter and the Cyrenians

Shelter was formed in the U.K. in 1966 from five charities which were trying to raise money for housing associations. Since then the charity has been the most important organisation for bringing pressure to bear on national and local government over the question of housing. It has also provided local advice for people seeking accommodation, looking for ways to improve their rented property or those in dispute with their landlords.

The Cyrenians bring together groups which have been set up to provide accommodation for homeless, single people. In some places the accommodation offered may take the form of night-shelters while in other places more long-term accommodation is provided. The intention of each centre, manned totally by volunteer help, is to provide accommodation for those people without a home, male or female. Each community is then expected to run itself, laying down basic ground-rules for its members and sharing out the decision-making process. In this way those people who have lost the habit of making decisions for themselves can, once again, begin to take control over their lives.

ANSWER IN YOUR BOOK ...

1 How serious a social problem is homelessness?
2 What are the basic amenities that should be available to everyone?
3 What is 'Shelter'?

FIND OUT AND NOTE ...

Homelessness is an international problem. While there are thought to be 3,000,000 people without adequate housing in the U.K., there are over 120,000,000 people worldwide. Try to find out about the following:

a) The homeless problem in the U.K. In particular:
  ❖ Who qualifies for housing benefit and who does not.
  ❖ Which groups in society are most vulnerable when it comes to substandard housing.
  ❖ Why homelessness has more than doubled in the last decade.

b) The homeless problem in other countries. In particular:
  ❖ The parts of the world in which the problem is most acute.
  ❖ The links between homelessness and such issues as poverty and war.

WHAT DO YOU THINK?

a) What do you think is the basic difference between a 'house' and a 'home'? What needs to be present to make them one in the same?

b) This quotation comes from the Church of England's Report 'Faith in the City':
"A home is more than having a roof over one's head. Decent housing certainly means a place that is warm and dry and in reasonable repair. It also means security, privacy, sufficient space, a place where people can grow and make choices…"
  ❖ How would you define 'decent housing'?
  ❖ What kind of social problems might prevent a person from treating a house as their 'home'?
  ❖ How do you think that substandard housing might affect a person's security, privacy and ability to grow as people?
  ❖ In what way might poor housing conditions affect a person's ability to make choices for themselves. Why would that be a bad thing?

3.8 THE DISABLED

Who are the 'disabled'? The word itself refers to the loss of the full use of any part of the human body. Under this umbrella-term are included the following:

1 *The mentally handicapped.* There are 500,000 people in the U.K. who are mentally disabled. MENCAP (The Royal Society for Mentally Handicapped Children and Adults) is the largest organisation in the U.K. specifically committed to looking after the interests of mentally disabled people.

2 *The physically disabled.* In the U.K. one in twelve people suffer from some kind of physical disability although the vast majority of these do not need specialist help. A large number of these people suffer from varying degrees of blindness or deafness.

Although there are about 1,200,000 disabled people in the U.K., about 60% of the world's disabled people live in developing countries. Many receive no other help apart from that offered by relatives and friends. Most have no chance of employment and many end up begging on the streets.

The International Year of the Disabled

In 1971 the United Nations set out the rights of mentally disabled people and in 1975 they did the same for the physically disabled. Then, in 1981, the United Nations led the way by declaring the International Year of the Disabled. It was given the motto 'Full participation and Equality'.

A *Do you think that disabled athletes and sports people should have as much public recognition as able-bodied ones? If so, why do you think this doesn't happen?*

Five objectives were set for the year. These remain the objectives of those trying to secure equal opportunities for all disabled people:

> **a)** To help physically and mentally disabled people become fully adjusted to life in society.
> **b)** To support all national and international efforts to train and educate disabled people to lead as full a life as possible. All disabled people have the right to full employment.
> **c)** To encourage shops and public places to make access for disabled people as easy as possible. This generally means installing ramps and special lifts.
> **d)** To educate the general public about the rights and needs of disabled people.
> **e)** To prevent disability as much as possible and to help in the physical and emotional rehabilitation of disabled people.

Why do you think that the International Year of the Disabled set itself the task of educating the able-bodied as well as meeting the needs of disabled people?

Helping the Disabled

There are many charities which have been set up to help the disabled. Most of them concentrate on one particular type of disability so that they are able to offer the specialised kind of help that is needed. From among this large number of societies we can mention just two – the Cheshire and Ryder Homes. Group Captain Leonard Cheshire was a hero of World War Two who wanted to do something useful with his life when the war ended. Starting in 1948, he set up a series of Homes to look after those who were chronically ill. By 1959 there were 23 of them in four different countries. By 1993 there were 270 such Homes in 51 different countries. In 1959, Cheshire married Sue Ryder and the Ryder-Cheshire Foundation set itself the task of exploring new ways of combatting suffering. This is now known as 'The Mission for the Relief of Suffering'.

B *What do you think are the basic needs of disabled people? Who should take the responsibility of trying to meet them?*

ANSWER IN YOUR BOOK ...

1 Who are the 'disabled'?

2 What were the objectives of the 'International Year of the Disabled' and why are these objectives still very important?

3 What do you think the basic needs are of disabled people?

FIND OUT AND NOTE ...

Try to find out about the following, according to the United Nations:

a) The rights of the mentally disabled.

b) The rights of the physically disabled.

How many of these Rights are recognised and granted in the U.K?

WHAT DO YOU THINK?

a) What do you think the United Nations meant by its motto 'Full participation and equality' for all kinds of disabled people?

b) Choose two of the objectives of the 'International Year of the Disabled' and explain, in your own words, what you think they mean in practice. Do you think that they have been achieved in the U.K?

c) Take a trip round your own locality. List what you see as the five most important needs that disabled people have. Try to find out what steps have been taken in your locality to meet these needs. Are there any needs which are clearly not being met?

d) Do you think that society does enough to meet the needs of the disabled? How high would you place the needs of the disabled on your list? What more could be done?

IN THE GLOSSARY ...

Developing Country.

3.9 OLD AGE

In the U.K. more and more people are surviving into old age. Look at the statistics about old age in the U.K for a moment:

1 There are now four times as many elderly people over the age of 65 in the U.K. than there were at the turn of the century. At the moment 17% of the population have reached retirement age compared with 6% in India and just over 3% in Brazil. One in every six adults in the U.K. has retired.
2 Life expectancy (the age to which a person can reasonably expect to live) is now 70 for a man and 75 for a woman.
3 The U.K. now has to support over 10,000,000 retired people. Those who do not work, including the elderly, must be supported by those who do.
4 A person in their seventies is 7 times more likely to visit their doctor than someone in their thirties.
5 By the year 2020 men and women in the U.K. will both retire at the same age – 65.

Think about these statistics for a moment. The prospect of an increasingly ageing population poses major problems for the future. Can you work out what some of these problems are?

Growing old – end or beginning?

Like everything else in life, growing old has a downside and an upside. Let us look at the downside first:

❖ There are three main problems associated with growing old:
   a) *Poverty.* Most elderly people experience a severe drop in income. Those entirely dependent on a State pension will inevitably find it very difficult to make ends meet.
   b) *Ill health.* Elderly people are more prone to chronic illnesses like arthritis, rheumatism and bronchitis. It also takes them longer to recover from everyday illnesses like the flu and a cold.
   c) *Loneliness.* Many people, especially women, have to face old age alone when their partners die. Over 2,000,000 elderly people in the U.K. live alone.

Now, let us look at the upside:

❖ Many old people actively enjoy their old age. Improved standards of healthcare mean that many more people are fit and healthy when they enter old age. Far from 'waiting to die' they find new

A Most people do not look forward to the idea of growing old with any great relish. What do you think they fear most about growing old?

interests. They now have much more time on their hands and this can be a great opportunity. They may take up new studies ('University of the Third Age'), travel or simply devote more time to hobbies such as gardening or painting. Old age can bring a sense of peace and tranquility. It should be a time when the worries, anxieties and struggles of the past are over. It can also be a time of reflection. For the Christian, old age should be a time of spiritual growth and preparation for the life to come.

B *Do elderly people need to be encouraged, or trained, to see retirement as a great opportunity?*

ANSWER IN YOUR BOOK ...

1 Why does an increasingly ageing population pose considerable problems for the future?

2 What are the major problems associated in most people's minds with growing old?

3 Why could old age be seen as a great opportunity?

READ AND DECIDE ...

In Biblical times, old people were always looked after within the extended family. This forms the background for what the Bible has to say about growing old. Read each of the following references with this in mind and then answer the questions:

a) **Exodus 20.12**
   What do you think 'honouring' means in practice when your parents are old?

b) **Exodus 21.12**
   Why do you think such a severe punishment was laid down for anyone who failed to fulfil their family responsibilities?

c) **Leviticus 19.32**
   This is concerned with showing respect for elderly people who do not belong to our family. What do you think that elderly people today could offer to society if society was prepared to listen?

d) **Mark 7.9-12**
   Jesus is complaining here about using the excuse of religious obligation to avoid showing respect to one's parents. What excuses do we sometimes use to avoid helping our parents?

e) **1.Timothy 5.4,8**
   How is the importance of looking after one's parents underlined here by Paul?

WHAT DO YOU THINK?

Here are three quotations about old age. In your own words, try to explain the point(s) that each of them is making:

a) **Graham Greene. 'A Sort of Life':**
   "With the approach of death I care less and less about religious truth. One hasn't long to wait for revelation and darkness."

b) **D.H.Lawrence. 'Selected Poems':**
   "It ought to be lovely to be old,
   To be full of the peace that comes from experience
   And wrinkled ripe fulfilment."

c) **Kokinshu. 'Anthology of Japanese Literature':**
   "If only, when one heard
   That Old-Age was coming
   One could bolt the door
   Answer 'Not at Home'
   And refuse to meet him."

3.10 AGEISM

Discrimination against the Elderly

Discrimination takes many forms in our society. We will be looking at sexual discrimination and racial discrimination elsewhere in the book. Both of these forms of discrimination have, quite rightly, received a considerable amount of publicity in recent years. Ageism is equally common – discrimination directed against people because they have reached a certain age. Consider the following:

a) Few people are given the choice as to whether they retire at a certain age or not. In the past the retirement pension has been paid to all men who reach their 65th birthday and to all women when they reach the age of 60. By the year 2020 the retirement age will be equalised for everyone at 65. Think about it for a moment or two. There is a certain assumption being made here. It is that few old people are able to do a satisfactory job of work and so need to be retired. Many may wish to do so but others would welcome the opportunity of continuing beyond retirement age, if only in a part-time capacity. For them the transition from full-time work to having unlimited spare time on their hands is all too sudden. What about introducing workers to the idea of retirement gradually? Is that a good idea or not?

b) Discrimination can lead to stereotyping. Stereotypes are 'fixed pictures' in the mind into which all people in a particular group must be fitted. Here are some typical stereotypes about old age:

> "Old people are always living in the past."
> "Old people never have a good word to say about young people. They are always criticising."
> "Old people are always a burden on their children and grandchildren."

You can see how unfair these statements are. Stereotypes are always unfair.

A Do you think that the elderly should be given the opportunity to continue working beyond retirement age if they want to?

Then and now

Things have certainly changed. In Biblical times the elderly were given the protection of their extended family until they died. Within that family there was a very strict hierarchy with the elderly parents at the top. They were always looked up to and respected for their experience and wisdom. They were consulted when all important family decisions were taken. As a result, the elderly felt that they still had a role to play in society.

That role has long since disappeared. Most elderly people now feel that there opinions are no longer valued. It is the younger members of the family who now take all the responsibility and make the decisions. By dispensing with the services of the elderly, and taking decisions on their behalf, we are contributing to ageism. Apart from the elderly in our own family, few of us have any kind of contact with the old people around us.

All of this could cause immense problems in the future. One in every six people in the U.K. is now elderly. By the year 2025 this will be reflected worldwide. Some way has to be found to look after them so that they can make a real contribution to the society in which they live.

B *How do you think elderly people could be encouraged to make a real contribution to society in the future?*

USE YOUR IMAGINATION ...

Over the years the United Nations has drawn up a list of 'rights' for the mentally and physically disabled, children and women. Imagine that you are on a committee given the responsibility of drawing up a list of 'Rights' for the elderly. What would you include on your list? We have begun the list to help you:

Rights For The Elderly

❖ Every elderly person should have the right to move around freely.
❖ Every elderly person should have the right to retain their independence for as long as possible.
❖ . . . .

a) Discuss and compare your list with two other people in your class. Try to draw up a 'Charter of Rights for the Elderly' which meets with the approval of most, if not all, members of your class.

b) Try to show the Charter to at least two elderly people, inside or outside your family, and make a note of their comments to contribute to a further class discussion.

FIND OUT AND NOTE ...

Many of the stereotypes that we hold about elderly people come from the mass media. During the next seven days collect as many newspaper cuttings as you can about old people and note down anything relevant from the television. How are the elderly portrayed by the mass media?

ANSWER IN YOUR BOOK ...

1 What is ageism?

2 What is stereotyping? Can you list five ways in which elderly people are often stereotyped in our society?

3 How do we treat elderly people today compared with Biblical times?

IN THE GLOSSARY ...

Sexual Discrimination; Racial Discrimination; Retirement Pension; Stereotyping.

4 LAW AND ORDER

Human beings are unique in that they are able to make independent moral choices. From the very beginning of the human race this has led to the formation of moral codes and laws. These laws form the foundation of every society. Usually, most people in a society obeys its laws and this makes it possible for people to live happily together. For various reasons, however, there will always be a small number of people who disobey the laws and threaten the stability of that society. Alongside the laws, therefore, a range of punishments are also needed. These are administered by people who are specially trained for the purpose – judges, prison officers, social workers, etc.

We live in a very complex society. You would expect, therefore, the code of law and the way that it is applied to be equally complicated. It is. It is very different, for example, to the laws in the period covered by both the Old and New Testaments. Life then was much simpler and the laws reflected this.

The Old Testament

The Jewish people based their whole way of life and religious beliefs on three basic principles:

a) That God was the Creator of the universe and of everything which lived within it. Human beings were simply 'stewards' of all that God had created.
b) That God was the Lord of history. Nothing happened which was not planned or designed by God.

A *In our society a person is considered innocent until they have been proved guilty. Why do you think that this is a very important principle of the criminal justice system?*

c) That God had made his will known to a group of people called the Jews. In particular, he had revealed his laws (called the ' Torah') to them when he appeared to Moses on Mount Sinai. Although there were 615 laws in all, covering a whole variety of ethical and ritual (religious) requirements, the laws were really summed up by the 'Ten Commandments'. You can refresh your memory of these by reading Exodus 20.1-17.

All of this happened at an early stage in Jewish history. In the centuries that followed the teachings of the various prophets added fresh demands and insights. A considerable amount of 'oral tradition' grew up alongside the books of the Torah relating the principles in the law to everyday situations.

The Jewish community itself was given the responsibility of carrying out God's will by punishing those who broke the laws. Many of these punishments were very harsh. The death penalty was frequently used. Those who blasphemed God's name and young people beyond the control of their parents, for example, were stoned to death. To make matters worse, those punished by a human court still had to face the judgement of God.

The New Testament

By the time of Jesus the ethical and the ritual codes had developed into separate systems. The people found it difficult to decide which was most important. When Jesus was asked about this he summed up the whole duty of human beings in words taken from the Old Testament books of Leviticus and Deuteronomy:

> "The first (commandment) is this, Hear, O Israel: the Lord our God is the one Lord, and you must love the Lord your God with all your heart, with all your soul, with all your mind and with all your strength." (Mark 12.29,30)

Jewish law was based upon a simple principle – that human beings owed their highest allegiance to God and so must deal fairly and justly with their fellow human beings. Jesus, however, did add a striking new feature. He emphasised compassion and forgiveness for those who had broken the law, as in the case of the woman caught in the very act of adultery (John 8.4). He also stressed the importance of inner motivation (Matthew 5.38-48). What do you think he meant by this?

ANSWER IN YOUR BOOK ...

1 Why are the laws and moral codes of a society so very important?

2 Which three principles formed the basis for the whole Jewish way of life and religion?

3 What new teaching did Jesus add to that in the Old Testament about the law and the way the criminal (law-breaker) should be treated?

DISCUSS AMONG YOURSELVES...

Here are four statements about dealing with those who break the law. Each of them has been mentioned in some way or other in this chapter. Discuss among yourselves whether you agree with them or not and make notes about your answers.

a) "Society deserves the criminals it gets and gets the criminals it deserves."

b) "If you punish a criminal violently then you create a violent society in return."

c) "It is quite impossible to be both merciful and just in dealing with the criminal. It is best to be on the safe side and deal with the criminal justly – forget the mercy."

d) "The Bible seems to support the idea of treating the criminal harshly – to act as a deterrent to others who might break the law. That seems sensible."

IN THE GLOSSARY ...

Old Testament; New Testament; Torah; Ten Commandments.

4.2 THE LAW – AND BREAKING IT

It is very difficult to escape the conclusion that there has been a 'crime explosion' in recent years. Let us look at some facts and figures:

a) In 1951 638,000 offences were reported to the Police in the U.K. and in 1971 this figure had risen to just over 1,9000,000. By 1986 it had reached almost 4,400,000 and by 1993 over 6,000,000 offences were reported each year. It is thought that for every crime reported at least three go unreported.

b) Men are seven times more likely than women to commit crimes.

c) Most crimes are committed by people under the age of 25, particularly those between the ages of 16 and 19.

d) While criminal activity has been traditionally associated with city areas, it has now spread far more to rural parts of the U.K.

What is the law?

There are two kinds of law in the U.K:

1 Laws which are passed by Parliament.
2 Bye-laws which are passed by local councils and cover such issues as trespass, parking, etc.

Bye-laws are intended to make life tolerable for everyone in their local area. They are administered by the Courts, just as the laws passed by Parliament are. These laws have built up over a long time. Even so, new laws are always being added and, occasionally, out-of-date laws are removed. To take just two examples:

❖ In 1967 the law covering homosexual behaviour in the U.K. was changed. For a long time such behaviour had been illegal. It is now legal under certain conditions.

❖ Barely sixty years ago people did not need to take a driving test before they were allowed to drive a car.

A Why do you think it has proved necessary to have more and more laws controlling the motor car? Are there any others that you would like to see?

Now a large number of offences are committed by car drivers. Laws are still being added to the statute book – such as the speed restriction placed on coaches on the motorway (58 m.p.h) to take effect in 1996 in the U.K.

The law, then, does not stand still. It grows and develops in keeping with changing conditions in society.

The law also varies from country to country. For example, the law forbids anyone in the U.K. to have more than one husband or wife at the same time. If they do so they are guilty of bigamy. In Muslim countries, however, a man is allowed to have more than one wife although the reverse is not the case. At the same time, most Muslim countries ban the sale or consumption of alcohol – a law which certainly does not apply in the U.K.

Breaking the law

As we have seen the law is broken frequently. Such law-breaking is divided into two categories:

❖ *Indictable offences* – the most serious kinds of crime including murder, manslaughter, rape, etc.

❖ *Non indictable offences* – such as petty theft, motoring offences, etc.

Why, though, do so many people break the law? Many suggested answers have been put forward:

a) *It is human nature.* All people are sinful and they express this trait of human nature by breaking the law.

b) *The Devil (Satan) leads people into temptation.* The increasing amount of crime in society reflects a breakdown in society's religious and moral standards.

c) *Home background and the stresses of modern life are to blame.* Unemployment leads directly to such criminal activities as drug-taking and vandalism.

d) *Greed.* We are all stimulated by advertisements to desire what we cannot afford. For many, crime is the only way of obtaining goods that are beyond their reach by any other means.

e) *The probability of getting away with it.* Less than 10% of crimes are solved. As long as they feel that they can get away with it, many people will resort to crime.

Can you shed any light on this very difficult question? Why do so many people break the law?

B *This is a very familiar sight in towns and cities within the U.K. Do you think that people would be less inclined to take the risk if the chance of them being caught was much higher?*

WHAT DO YOU THINK?

There is so much that is confusing about crime and the law in the U.K. Discuss the following issues with other people in your class and try to come up with some explanations:

a) Why are men much more likely than women to commit a crime?

b) Why are more and more crimes being committed in rural areas of the U.K?

c) Why are such a high proportion of crimes being committed by young people, especially those between the ages of 16 and 19.

ANSWER IN YOUR BOOK ...

1 What are the different kinds of law in the U.K?

2 What is the difference between an indictable and a non-indictable offence?

3 Why do people break the law?

READ AND DECIDE ...

Jewish and Christian views of right and wrong are based, to a greater or lesser extent, on the Ten Commandments. Read these for yourself in Exodus 20.3-17.

a) How many of these Commandments do you think still apply to life in the 20th century?

b) Write your own list of Commandments for today. Incorporate any of the Ten Commandments in your list if you think they are still appropriate.

No Parking
Motorists failing to comply with parking restrictions on Railway property are liable to prosecution under Byelaw 25

C *How would you explain the difference between laws passed by parliament and bye-laws such as the one illustrated here?*

IN THE GLOSSARY ...

Bye-law; Homosexual; Muslim; Devil; Satan.

4.3 PUNISHMENT

Anyone found guilty of committing a crime in the U.K. will be punished by a court of law. For minor offences, a fine or probation is the usual punishment. For more serious offences, a criminal may be sent to prison for any length of time from a few days to life. In the case of a life sentence a judge may recommend that a minimum sentence be served. In some extreme cases, such as the child murderers Ian Brady and Myra Hindley, life can now literally mean a life in prison.

What is punishment all about? What is society trying to accomplish when it sentences a criminal? What kinds of punishment are appropriate for the crimes committed? A person is usually punished for four reasons:

a) *Retribution*. This can quite simply be defined as making a person pay for what they have done. In some cases, this can be taken to extreme lengths. A few years ago a judge in South Carolina, U.S.A., offered a rapist the choice between castration and going to prison. This prompted the 'New York

Times' to ask the question:

> "Why not offer pickpockets the choice between prison and amputation or threaten 'Peeping Toms' with blindness?"

Some countries certainly carry out much harsher punishments than others. Many, including certain States in the U.S.A, carry the death penalty for serious crimes like murder. In Muslim countries a thief might have his or her hand cut off in keeping with the teaching of the Holy Scriptures, the Quran.

b) *Protection*. Most people accept that society needs real protection against people who threaten it. Locking a criminal away means that he or she cannot endanger life or property. Of course, when they are released it might be a different story. Three out of every four people who spend some time in prison re-offend.

A *Do these headlines suggest that society is winning the battle against crime or not?*

The killers who will never go free

Murdered doctor was pestered by obsessive man

Life for arsonist who killed 11 at sex cinema

Five held as 3,000 protest at Criminal Justice Act

ael Smith

Childminde who killed jailed 4 year

Killer seeks to overturn 'jail until death' tern

Woman, 80, relives rape ordeal

Doctor beaten up for no-smoking reminder

Police dawn raids net 911 burglary suspects

Courts get new power to lock up children

Father 'started fire that killed his 3 children'

'Model pupil' raped girl after chase

Victims cheer as rapist gets four life sentences

Mother kills three children

Man jailed for pullin out baby' toenails

Father set on fire by teenage gang

Accused Briton faces beating before death

Bring back flogging to curb young, says judge

c) *Deterrent.* Punishment is intended to discourage offenders from committing any further crimes and to make an example of them so that others will find crime less attractive. In truth, the theory does not seem to work since there is a high chance that people will return to prison.

d) *Reform.* Prison should be used to try to change the criminal so that they no longer want to commit crime. This is particularly important for young offenders. Over 200,000 young offenders (juvenile delinquents – under the age of 19) go through the courts every year in the U.K. and a high proportion of these carry on leading a life of crime. Prisons in the U.K. today are very overcrowded. This makes the business of reforming the criminal very difficult. About 45,000 people in prison occupy space that was built for a population of less than 28,000.

B This notice is placed outside a Salvation Army shop in an inner-city area. Do you think that punishment is the best way of dealing with crime in such an area?

The Bible and punishment

The Christian approach is to steer a path between punishment and forgiveness. In the Old Testament punishment alone was stressed:

> "If one person strikes another and kills him, he must be put to death … If anyone injures and disfigures a fellow-countryman it must be done to him as he has done: fracture for fracture, eye for eye, tooth for tooth" (Leviticus 24.17-19)

In the New Testament the emphasis is placed upon non-violence and forgiveness. While not directly repudiating the teaching of the Old Testament, Jesus suggested that there was a better way. This was the way of non-violence as you can discover from Matthew 5.38-39. Jesus encouraged his followers not to judge other people in case the same standards were applied against them (Matthew 7.1). When Jesus was on the cross suffering the ultimate punishment for a crime that he did not commit he asked that others might be forgiven – Luke 23.34. How do you think these principles should be applied to the whole concept of punishment?

ANSWER IN YOUR BOOK …

1 What is society basically setting out to do when it punishes a criminal?

2 In what way is it hoped that punishment might deter the criminal?

3 Why is it very difficult to use prison as the place to reform the criminal?

CAN YOU EXPLAIN?

a) Can you outline the four distinct aims of punishment. Try to find some examples from your newspapers, or on television, to illustrate each of these aims.

b) Can you explain what you think is meant by 'retribution'? Do you think that a modern society should try to exact retribution from someone who has broken its laws?

c) Can you explain whether or not you think that stiff penalties stop people from committing crimes?

d) How important do you think it is to try to reform the criminal while he or she is in custody? Can you explain why this seldom seems to happen with our present system?

e) Can you explain how Christianity tries to maintain a balance between punishment and forgiveness in approaching the criminal?

f) Do you think that people who have broken the law should be offered a chance to redeem themselves? What about people who have been told that they will spend the rest of their lives in prison?

IN THE GLOSSARY …

Probation; Juvenile Delinquent; Old Testament; New Testament.

4.4 PRISON

Faced with the need to pass sentence on someone who has been found guilty of a serious crime, a judge needs to consider whether a 'custodial' (prison) sentence is appropriate. There are some 28,000 prison places available in the U.K. but, at any given time, the prison population is likely to exceed 45,000. Of this number just 2000 are women. The U.K. locks away more people than any other country in Western Europe. It costs over £300 a week to keep a prisoner in jail and the prison service costs some £750,000,000 (£750 million) a year to run.

A *Do you think that a long sentence in a place like Dartmoor is an effective way of treating those people who have broken the law?*

Why prison?

The U.K. has been locking people away in prison as a form of punishment for about 200 years. Although several new prisons have come into operation in recent years, and others are in the pipeline, most of our prisons are very old. Two main questions have been asked about sending people to prison:

1 What are the purposes of locking people up for a long period of time?
2 Is our prison service geared towards accomplishing these purposes?

Let us first look at the reasons why people are sent to prison.

a) *To keep law-abiding citizens safe from those who would otherwise threaten them.* Prisoners breaking out of jail may make the headlines but this is a comparatively rare occurrence. In the main, society is a safer place because the worst villains have been locked away.

B *Do you think that prisons such as this have a real deterrent value? If not, would you like to see any changes made?*

b) *To deter people from committing crime.* At one time in the U.K. the Death Penalty was the 'ultimate deterrent' but that has been abolished. The most serious deterrent is now a long spell in prison. Few criminals, however, spend longer than 12 years inside and many people argue that this destroys the deterrent value of a prison sentence. They argue that sentences should be longer although that would require more prison places. What do you think?

c) *To educate and reform the criminal.* Although prisons now provide educational and counselling facilities for the prisoners the emphasis is very much on containment rather than reformation. This is bad news from society's point of view. It can only hope that the criminal will come out of prison a reformed character. Unfortunately, 75% of those sentenced to prison return for a second sentence. These people are called 'recidivists'. This fact alone suggests that the prison service is failing.

There is another major flaw with the prison system in the U.K. At any given time there are thousands of people in prison who have not been brought before a court and found guilty. Such people are those who are on 'remand'. This means that they have been charged with an offence, brought before a court and sentenced to be 'remanded in custody' until their case can be tried. Sometimes they spend up to twelve months in custody before their case is heard. A considerable number are then found not guilty and released. Civil Rights groups argue that this is intolerable.

ANSWER IN YOUR BOOK ...

1 What do you think are the main reasons for sending a criminal to jail?

2 Would you like to see more criminals sent to jail as has been happening in recent years?

3 What is the evidence to suggest that sending people to prision is a very expensive and pretty ineffective form of punishment?

CAN YOU EXPLAIN?

The writers of the books of the New Testament often expressed an interest in the welfare of those who were confined to prison. Here is one such comment:

"Remember those in prison, as if you were there with them, and those who are being maltreated, for you are vulnerable too." (Hebrews 13.3)

What kind of sympathy do you think that Christians today should feel for those who are locked up in prison?

USE YOUR IMAGINATION ...

Can you remember the aims of punishment that we looked at in Unit 4.3? If not, refresh your memory. Imagine that you could design a prison and install a regime which allowed you to put these aims in to practice:

a) What features would you build into your prison so that these aims could be achieved?

b) How would you choose and train staff so that they could play a constructive role in prison life?

c) Explain how you would do the following:
- ❖ guarantee that prisoners were kept safely within the prison and had no opportunity to escape;
- ❖ build a system so that prisoners had the opportunity to engage in constructive work;
- ❖ help prisoners to see that a life of crime only caused personal and social distress;
- ❖ help prisoners to build up real hope for their future life outside prison.

You might like to spend some time discussing these issues with the rest of the class before you put pen to paper.

4.5 CAPITAL PUNISHMENT

The practice of putting people to death for committing certain crimes is not new. The Romans crucified all criminals who were not Roman citizens and beheaded those who were. In 18th century Britain a person could be put to death for any one of over 200 different offences. These included stealing a loaf of bread or taking someone's sheep. In the years that followed there were a number of reforms and punishments became less severe. The Death Penalty, however, remained for most forms of murder until 1957 when Parliament restricted capital punishment to:

❖ killing during an armed robbery;
❖ killing a policeman;
❖ killing by explosion;
❖ killing more than one person.

In 1965 Parliament suspended the Death Penalty for a trial period of five years and in 1970 it was abolished altogether.

For and against Capital Punishment

It is now many years since the Death Penalty was abolished in the U.K. Several attempts have been made in Parliament to bring it back for certain kinds of crime but they have been unsuccessful. What are the main arguments put forward on both sides of the debate?

a) **For:**
❖ Capital Punishment is a tried and tested way of dealing with murderers based on the principle from the Old Testament of 'an eye for an eye and a tooth for a tooth'.
❖ Unfortunately, some people in our society only understand the language of violence. Capital Punishment is the only deterrent that has any effect on the way that people behave.
❖ Society has a duty to protect those in the front line of the fight against crime such as the police, prison

A *The death penalty has been reintroduced by some of the States in the U.S.A. This protest is against an execution being carried out. Who do you think has the strongest case in this particular argument?*

wardens, etc. It also must protect those who cannot protect themselves. This includes children, old people, etc.

❖ A 'life sentence' may be no longer than ten years. When the prisoner is released there are no guarantees that he or she won't murder again.

❖ The Death Penalty means that justice can be seen to be done. The family and friends of a murdered person have the right to demand retribution.

b) Against:

❖ Only God has the right to give and take life.

❖ How can we ever be sure that someone is guilty? We now know of several people who have been executed this century in the U.K. for crimes they did not commit.

❖ There is no conclusive evidence that the Death Penalty is an effective deterrent to anyone intent on killing. In New York, for instance, where the Death Penalty is used, the murder rate is 14 times higher than that in the U.K.

❖ Executing terrorists would turn them into martyrs and provoke further atrocities.

❖ The Death Penalty is barbaric. Most enlightened countries have abolished it. Those countries which still have Capital Punishment are often condemned for inhumane treatment. The Death Penalty remains in over 100 countries in the world. Many executions are carried out in secret but it is thought that

between 10,000 and 40,000 executions have been performed since 1980. Amnesty International is at the forefront of organisations and pressure groups trying to change this situation.

ANSWER IN YOUR BOOK ...

1 What is Capital Punishment?

2 When was Capital Punishment abandoned in the U.K?

3 Do you think there would be less serious crime in the U.K. if the Death Penalty existed?

READ AND DECIDE ...

Amnesty International has declared that the Death Penalty is a violent denial of a person's human rights. In December 1977 it stated that Capital Punishment is:
   "...the ultimate cruel, inhuman and degrading punishment which violates the right to life..."

It went on to add the following:

a) Execution is an act of violence and violence always leads to more violence. Do you agree with this?

b) Everyone involved in putting someone to death is degraded and brutalised. Would you be happy to be involved in the process?

c) Execution does not allow time for reflection and sometimes the innocent are killed. Can you find any examples of this?

WHAT DO YOU THINK?

Until the Death Penalty was abolished in the U.K. an announcement was always nailed to the prison gate after an execution had been carried out. Crowds of people waited to read the announcement. What do you think they were doing there?

COMPLETE A CHART ...

Draw up a list of arguments for and against the Death Penalty in the form of a chart like this:

THE DEATH PENALTY

Arguments for:
1
2
3

Arguments against:
1
2
3

Which arguments do you find to be most convincing? Add any further arguments of your own to either side?

4.6 DOMESTIC VIOLENCE

We hardly need the crime statistics which are published each year to tell us that our society is becoming more and more violent. Crimes such as murder, manslaughter, grievous bodily harm and rape have steadily risen over the last decade. So, too, has 'domestic violence'.

Violence in the home

Domestic violence is not a new problem. In the past, however, most women had little option but to stay with their husbands, no matter how badly they were treated. Few of them had any hope of surviving on their own. In this respect, things have changed. Major changes in the law concerning sexual equality and equal pay for women (1975) as well as changes in the property laws gave women real financial independence. For a long time women have been able to divorce their husbands on equal grounds. The Women's Movement (often called the 'Feminist Movement') has encouraged thousands of women to move towards independence.

Yet violence is still a feature of many marriages. Experience teaches us that thousands of women are still subjected to humiliating and violent treatment from their husbands – psychological as well as physical abuse. Excessive drinking often plays a major role in the behaviour of violent men. Battered women often turn to doctors, social workers or the Police for help. These agencies, however, were, until recently, reluctant to become involved in domestic matters.

This situation is gradually changing. The extent of domestic violence is now being recognised by everyone. Various Women's Aid Refuges have emerged which, as their name suggests, offer a safe 'refuge' for women from the violence. What, then, do battered women need?

a) They need protection. They need to be in a place where their partner cannot reach them. This is the first priority.

b) They need to regain their self-confidence and self-respect. When they arrive in a refuge they discover that other women also experience the same problems as themselves. Together they begin to

A This refuge for battered wives offers help and care for women who have suffered violence at the hands of their partners. Why do you think that domestic violence is such a problem?

build up each other's self-esteem and confidence. On their own they might seem powerless against a violent husband but together they find added strength.

c) They need to regain control over their lives. On the receiving end of constant abuse and violence, they have lost control of their lives. Taking responsibility for the running of the refuge, they gradually begin to make decisions for themselves again.

d) They need to know whether leaving home is practical and, if so, how they go about it. How do they claim social security, housing benefit or benefits for their children? All these are very practical matters but they may well have a considerable bearing on future decisions that need to be taken.

Refuges, then, are essential in a society which sees an increasing number of men using violence against their partners and children. Although almost all of these refuges are set up and maintained by voluntary contributions, they now have the support of a growing number of doctors and social workers. They recognise the enormous contribution that these hostels make towards solving a very serious social problem. In the long-term, however, the answer must lie in helping people to see that violence is not the answer to any problem. Violent men need as much help, in their own way, as do battered women.

ANSWER IN YOUR BOOK ...

1 How is the increasing amount of violence in our society reflected in the home?

2 What do women who suffer from continual violence from their partners need most of all?

3 What kind of help and support is provided by Women's Aid refuges?

READ AND DECIDE ...

For a man of his period Jesus showed quite extraordinary compassion towards women. Look up the following references and make notes on them:

a) Mark 12.40

b) Mark 10.10-12

c) Luke 7.36-49

d) John 8.1-11

Sum up, in about 400 words, the attitude of Jesus towards women who suffered.

WHAT DO YOU THINK?

You discover that a married friend of yours has been using violence against his wife. What would you try to do about it? What kind of help do you think he would need?

5.1 DRUGS – THE FACTS

Drug-taking or substance abuse affects the whole of society. Such substances range from tranquilisers or sleeping pills to serious (hard) drugs such as cocaine. 4,000,000 sleeping pills, for example, are taken each night in the U.K. and 500,000 people are thought to be addicted to these substances. That, however, is a separate problem.

Here, we will concentrate on those substances which are not prescribed by a doctor (illegal substance abuse). First, let us look at some general information about drugs.

Drugs – the facts

A drug is any substance which effects the chemistry of the body when it is injected, swallowed, smoked or inhaled. It also upsets the delicate balance which exists between the body and the mind. Once taken it rapidly passes into the bloodstream. It is then carried to the brain where it acts on the central nervous system. It affects a person's moods, behaviour, speech, sight and physical condition.

Tobacco and alcohol are the two most commonly used drugs in our society. We will take a look at them more closely in Units 5.3 and 5.5. Here we just note that:

a) 100,000 people in the U.K. die prematurely each year as a direct result of smoking;
b) 700,000 people in the U.K. are thought to have a serious drinking problem.

In terms of sheer numbers, smoking and drinking alcohol represent a far more serious threat to the nation's health than illegal drug abuse. The illegal use of drugs, however, is a major problem and one that is rapidly getting worse.

Such drugs can be classified as follows:

1 *Amphetamines (speed)*. These stimulate the body and its reactions, making a person excited and over-active. Depression follows. Taken over a long period amphetamines can lead to heart problems, malnutrition and death.
2 *Cannabis (pot)*. Heightens the awareness of our senses. Pot can lead to hallucinations and confusion. It may also damage lung tissues.

A Why do you think that more and more people are turning to the illegal use of drugs?

B Why do you think so many people in our society need to take tranquilisers and sleeping pills?

Drug Abuse

'Drug abuse' takes place whenever a person allows a substance into their body which has not been prescribed by their doctor. If they then take enough of that substance over a period of time, they become dependent on it. Such dependency can take one of two forms:

a) *A physical dependence*. This happens when a person experiences a physical craving for the substance when it is withheld. Tranquilisers, cigarettes, alcohol and even coffee are capable of producing this element of dependence. As the body becomes used to the substance, more will be needed to produce the desired feelings and sensations.

b) *A psychological dependence*. This happens when a person 'feels' that they cannot cope without the substance. Most 'drug dependence' has a physical and a psychological element. A state of 'drug addiction' is reached when a person's body cannot manage without the substance. If that substance is withdrawn very unpleasant side-effects can take place.

3 *LSD (acid)*. Leads to hallucinations and feelings of panic. These may continue after a person stops taking the drug.

4 *Cocaine (coke)*. Acts like amphetamines but is more likely to lead to dependence. Withdrawal can be very painful and unpleasant.

5 *Heroin (smack)*. Produces lethargy, apathy, loss of judgement and self-control. Since heroin is usually injected, users risk contracting hepatitis or AIDS if they share dirty needles.

6 *Crack and Ecstasy*. These have only arrived on the scene comparatively recently. Crack has a similar effect to cocaine but can cause brain damage or sudden death. Ecstasy causes confusion and paranoia.

ANSWER IN YOUR BOOK ...

1 How would you define a drug?

2 How do drugs affect the body?

3 What are the main types of drugs?

IN YOUR OWN WORDS ...

Define each of the following terms in your own words:

a) Drug abuse

b) Drug dependency

c) Drug addiction

FIND OUT AND NOTE ...

Find out as much as you can about the following:

a) Amphetamines   d) Heroin
b) Cannabis   e) Ecstasy
c) Cocaine   f) Crack

Present your information in the form of a table with the following headings:

Drug	Substance	Appearance	How taken	Effects

IN THE GLOSSARY ...

Drug Abuse; Drug Dependency; Drug Addiction.

5.2 DRUGS – THE EFFECTS

Drug-taking is a complex problem. A whole range of factors may lead a person to become involved with drugs. They include the following:

a) *Boredom* – 'I did it for kicks'.
b) *Peer Pressure* – 'Everyone else does it so…'
c) *Anxiety and tension* – 'It helps me relax, have a good time and forget about all my problems.'
d) *Personal problems* – 'It makes me feel better about myself and that is important.'
e) *Novelty* – 'You know me, I'll try anything once.'
f) *Rebellion* – 'If my parents are so strongly against drugs then I will take them. It is a way of getting back at them and all they stand for.'

The dangers of substance abuse

Few people, when they take drugs for the first time, are aware of the risks that they run. The risks are somewhat different depending on the substance taken but drugs:

- …can cause depression, heart problems and malnutrition;
- …can lead to confusion and hallucinations;
- …can cause permanent injury to the liver, lungs and brain;
- …can lead to chronic constipation and a disruption of the menstrual cycle;
- …can affect a person's mental health;
- …can lead to jaundice and blood poisoning or even the transmission of the HIV virus;
- …can result in premature death.

Drug-taking often destroys personal relationships and breaks links with friends and family. Drugs are also

A *Do you think that the situation today with drugs in the U.K. is a cause for concern? Give reasons for your answer.*

Peer's 20-year fight to save addict sis
Boy made £2...,00 from heroin sales
Drug groups condemn Channel 4 cannabis night
Suicide bid after drug error
Does smoking pot damage your health?
LEGALISE IT.. ALL OF IT
'Ram' raids finance the drug deals of criminal underworld
Court frees drugs doctor
Cocaine cartels in control as Mexico markets face meltdown
Legalise pot, says head of youth agency
Boy died of thirst after parents took overdose
fights drug verdict
Girl, 19, died in New Age drug pact
Mother killed son fearing he would become an addict
'Dad's gone, Mum's a junkie' drug-ridder
Gun ambush victim linked to drug war
Drug barons reap rich rewards from rave scene
Viewers call for legal cannabis
Drug witnesses offered new lives
Heroin addict tells how eight hits a day ruined his career
Sellers daughter jailed for US drug offence
drugs
Drugs blamed for huge rise in murder rate
Comedian's son died a drug addict

very expensive. Many of those who are heavily into drugs find that they cannot hold down a regular job. Instead, they are forced to steal to finance their habit.

Withdrawal

Some 80 hospitals in the U.K. have facilities to help people who are addicted to drugs. A few of these provide in-patient care but the majority offer Drug Dependency Clinics. A person may attend these sessions voluntarily, after a referral from their own doctor, or be compelled to attend by a court order. When someone attends such a clinic for the first time they are given a thorough medical examination with blood and urine samples being taken. When the addict's needs have been assessed, treatment can then get underway. This will take one of two forms:

1 Usually he or she is 'weaned off' the drug with supplies being cut down gradually or with a substitute drug being prescribed which is less dangerous. Heroin addicts, for example, may be prescribed methadone.

2 Instant withdrawal (cold turkey), when the addict simply stops taking the drug. This approach can be effective but the person usually suffers severe withdrawal symptoms. The nature of these symptoms will depend on the drug they have been taking and the severity of their addiction.

Whatever method of treatment is chosen, a person will need a great deal of support and care. This is often supplied within a community and many such communities have a Christian basis. They are concerned with helping the addict through the traumas of withdrawal but also with the vitally important business of providing care afterwards. Two such centres in the U.K. are:

a) *Yeldall Manor, Reading* – this was set up in 1977 to help male addicts between the ages of 18 and 35. It provides care within an atmosphere of love and discipline. Underlying this is the belief that commitment to God and Christ can help overcome the addiction.

b) *Coke Hall Trust, Hampshire* – this accepts men and women between the ages of 20 and 35. People are expected to be drug-free when they enter and they are helped to begin to put their lives together again.

ANSWER IN YOUR BOOK ...

1 What kind of pressures could lead a person to take drugs?

2 What problems can be caused by drug-taking?

3 How are many Christians involved in trying to help people with their drug problems?

WHAT DO YOU THINK?

a) Do you think that a form of treatment which offers a combination of physical, social and religious support may have something to offer to drug addicts?

b) Do you think that the Christian religion has anything to offer addicts? If so, what do you think that might be?

c) Why do you think that Christian organisations, and individual Christian believers, have always been in the forefront of the fight against drugs?

READ AND DECIDE ...

Read these two verses from one of Paul's letters carefully:

"Surely you know that you are God's temple, where the Spirit of God dwells. Anyone who destroys God's temple will himself be destroyed by God, because the temple of God is holy; and you are that temple." (1.Corinthians 3.16-17)

a) What does Paul describe here by the phrase 'God's temple'?

b) What does Paul say will happen to anyone responsible for destroying God's temple?

c) What do you think these verses may have to say about taking drugs and addiction in general?

IN THE GLOSSARY ...

HIV.

5.3 SMOKING

Tobacco is thought to have reached British shores during the 16th century through Sir Walter Raleigh. It is now a highly sophisticated industry affecting some 35% of the adult population directly and the remaining 65% indirectly (through 'passive smoking').

Smoking and health

There are over 40 different poisonous substances in each cigarette including nicotine, tar and carbon monoxide. As a person inhales, a mixture of these chemicals enter the blood-stream. The carbon monoxide prevents the body from getting its normal supply of oxygen while the nicotine speeds up the heart-rate. Over time, deposits of tar collect in the air passages and affect the lungs.

Each year over 50,000 people die in the U.K. from illnesses directly related to cigarette smoking. This figure is 800% greater than the number killed in road accidents. The most common causes of death among smokers are the following:

1 *Coronary heart disease.* Each year 40,000 people in the U.K. under the age of 65 die from heart disease. Some 75% of these deaths are linked to smoking.

2 *Cancer.* 50 people a day in the U.K. die from lung cancer and 90% of these have been heavy smokers. The nicotine and tar in cigarettes are carcinogenic – i.e: they create the necessary conditions which lead to cancer.

3 *Bronchitis and emphysema.* A 'smoker's cough' is a frightening condition. It makes people fight to gain their breath. In many cases such chest conditions prove fatal.

In money terms smoking costs the National Health Service in the U.K. about £200,000,000 a year. Add to that the cost to employers and families and it becomes clear that smoking is a very costly habit for everyone involved.

There is another, more disturbing, cost. 'Passive smoking' is inhaling someone else's cigarette smoke. Anyone who lives or works with a heavy smoker inevitably inhales some of their smoke. Some doctors suggest that passive smoking kills as many as 1000 people every year in the U.K. Recently, a campaign was launched to ban smoking in all public places such as buses, offices and shops. Do you think that would be a good idea?

A Do you think that more trouble should be taken to prevent people from smoking, especially in public places?

B This advertisement is displayed within 200 yards of a school. Do you think that its position is coincidental? Do you think that such advertisements should be banned so close to schools, as the British Government proposed in 1994?

Happines
is a cigar
called
Hamlet.

Hamlet
MILD CIGARS

SMOKING CAUSES FATAL DISEASES

Giving up

Nicotine is addictive. Many people try hard to give up and fail repeatedly. Heavy smokers, like other 'drug addicts', will experience 'withdrawal symptoms' if they try to stop. They may suffer from stress, put on weight or become tired and irritable.

WHAT DO YOU THINK?

Here are some controversial opinions about smoking and its effect upon health. Produce as many arguments as you can for and against the opinions being expressed.

a) "The cigarette is the most lethal instrument devised by man for peaceful use."

b) "Smoking should be banned in all public places including transport, work-places, restaurants and sports arenas."

c) "Everyone taken to hospital for a smoking related illness should be turned away – or made to pay for their treatment."

d) "It's a free country – or supposed to be. If a person wants to smoke they should be free to do so – no matter what effect it has on their health or anyone else's."

e) "These days everything seems to be bad for your health. We are always being told about pollution, our eating habits, the perils of drink and now smoking. I wish the do-gooders would stop interfering in my life."

Helpful strategies for the determined person might be the following:

a) To use a substitute – such as herbal cigarettes or chewing gum.
b) To find alternative ways of relaxing.
c) To avoid situations and places where other people smoke.
d) To award oneself a treat when certain goals and objectives have been reached.
e) To begin to appreciate the benefits of giving up such as a better sense of taste and smell.
f) To use hypnosis or some similar technique.

ANSWER IN YOUR BOOK ...

1 What happens if a person inhales the smoke from a cigarette?

2 What are the most common causes of death among cigarette smokers?

3 What is passive smoking and how dangerous is it?

DISCUSS AMONG YOURSELVES...

The argument against smokers has been summed up in the following way:

"Smokers are very selfish people who think only of themselves."

Do you agree with this statement?

5.4 ALCOHOL – THE FACTS

No-one knows exactly when people first discovered how to produce alcohol. It was certainly well-known to the ancient Greeks and Romans, the latter having a god of wine called 'Bacchus'. The Epic of Gilgamesh, written in Babylonia in about 2225 BC, had this to say about alcohol:

> "Sweet drink put far away their cares. As they drank liquor their bodies became satiated. Much they bubbled and their mood was exalted."

In the Jewish Scriptures the first record of alcohol is found in Genesis where, we are told, Noah planted a vineyard, drank the wine and became drunk (Genesis 9.21). There were many excellent vineyards in Israel and wine was often drunk instead of the easily contaminated water supply. Wine was also used to relieve pain and was highly valued for its ability to help people forget their problems (Judges 9.13). Yet, even then, the ravages of over-drinking were well recognised:

> "Do not keep company with drunkards or those who are greedy for the fleshpots. The drunkard and the glutton will end in poverty; in a state of stupor they are reduced to rags." (Proverbs 23.20)

If a man wanted to show his total dedication to God he took a Nazarite Vow. Samson, in the Old Testament, and John the Baptist, in the New, took the vow. Any man who did this swore that any strong drink would not cross his lips. Yet, as the Gospels show, wine was widely used in New Testament times. Jesus turned water into wine at a wedding feast (John 2.3-10) although we cannot be sure that this event actually took place. The other Gospels, though, take wine for granted and the drinking of it is at the centre of the most important act of Christian worship – Holy Communion.

The effect of alcohol

Alcohol is not, contrary to public opinion, a stimulant. It is a depressant. Within 30 seconds of consuming it, the alcohol reaches the brain and begins to affect the various organs of the body. When drunk heavily and regularly alcohol has the following effects:

a) *It slows the brain down.* This affects reaction time, judgement and self-control. It also changes moods, speech, sight and balance.
b) *It poisons the liver.* This essential organ can cope with small quantities of alcohol (which are not harmful) but too much alcohol, over an extended period, will damage it permanently. The most common cause of death among very heavy drinkers is cirrhosis of the liver.
c) *It damages the heart.* In damaging and weakening the heart muscle, alcohol increases the risk of a heart attack by building up fatty deposits around

A Why do you think that anyone who took the Nazarite Vow was expected to refuse to drink any alcohol?

the heart. Even a small amount of alcohol increases blood pressure and causes a faster pulse rate, putting additional strain on the heart.

d) *It affects the stomach.* While small quantities of alcohol can help the stomach digest food, large quantities, over a period of time, can cause cancer, stomach ulcers and muscle wastage.

There is more about alcohol abuse in Unit 5.5. Here we simply point out that there is much debate among Christians over alcohol. The great temperance movements of the 19th century showed clearly how strongly both Protestants and Roman Catholics felt about the evils of drink. Members of the Methodist Church, for example, were encouraged to sign the Pledge at a very young age. In the 20th century, however, the Methodist Church has altered its strong anti-alcohol stance and the only Christian Church which now demands teetotalism of its members is the Salvation Army.

B *Alcohol can now be bought from supermarkets, off licences and pubs. Do you think we have made it too easy for people, especially teenagers, to obtain it?*

ANSWER IN YOUR BOOK ...

1 What was the attitude of the writers of the Old Testament towards alcohol?

2 What effect does alcohol have on the body?

3 What have been the attitudes of the Methodist Church and the Salvation Army towards alcohol?

WRITE AN ESSAY ...

Here is a list of references in the Bible to alcohol, drinking and drunkenness. Read them through carefully and make some notes in your book:

Leviticus 10.9; Judges 13.4; Numbers 6.3,20; Proverbs 23.19-21; Exodus 32.1-6; John 2.1-11; Romans 13.13; 1.Timothy 5.23; 3.2-3; Ephesians 5.18.

Now write an essay of 500 words with the title: 'The Bible, alcohol and drunkenness.'

WHAT DO YOU THINK?

Here are two very old comments about alcohol. Read them carefully:

a) A Japanese proverb:
"First the man takes the drink, then the drink takes a drink, then the drink takes the man."

b) Proverbs 23.29-32:
"Whose is the misery? Whose the remorse?
Whose are the quarrels and the anxiety?
Who gets the bruises without knowing why?
Whose eyes are bloodshot?
Those who linger late over their wine,
those always sampling some new spiced liquor."

"Do not gulp down the wine, the strong red wine,
when the droplets form on the side of the cup.
It may flow smoothly
but in the end it will bite like a snake
and poison like a cobra."

Write a warning against the dangers of drinking too much alcohol based upon these two quotations.

IN THE GLOSSARY ...

Nazarite Vow; John The Baptist; Old Testament; New Testament; Holy Communion; Temperance Movement; Protestant; Roman Catholic Church; Methodist Church; Pledge; Salvation Army; Teetotaller.

5.5 ALCOHOL – THE CONSEQUENCES

According to the World Health Organisation, 7% of the world's population is now dependent on alcohol. There is nothing new about this . As we saw in Unit 5.4, writers in the Old Testament rejoiced in God's gift of the vine and then warned their readers that alcohol will '…bite like a snake and poison like a cobra' (Proverbs 23.32). Drunkenness has been a problem in almost every society in which alcohol has been freely available. Heavy drinking causes a wide range of related problems. These include the following:

a) *Drink and driving.* Even very small amounts of alcohol impair a driver's judgement. Although there has been some improvement in recent years, alcohol is still the cause of more than 50% of serious road accidents.

b) *Drink and crime.* Chief Police Officers say that alcohol is directly responsible for a large number of crimes, particularly murder and rape. Reports suggest that some 25% of juveniles in detention centres have a serious drink problem. Drink is also a major factor in the behaviour of over 60% of petty criminals who return to prison on more than one occasion.

c) *Drink and work.* In the U.K. 14,000,000 working days are lost each year through absence from work due to drink-related problems.

d) *Drink and violence.* It is estimated that over 50% of reported cases of domestic violence and wife-battering are due to excessive drinking. Over 60% of all child cruelty occurs after someone, usually the father, has been drinking heavily.

e) *Drink and family life.* Nine out of every ten 13 year olds in the U.K. have tasted alcohol. An alarming number of young people are seriously addicted to alcohol by the time they reach their 18th birthday. Excessive drinking is also a major factor in the break-up of many marriages.

f) *Drink and death.* The excessive drinking of alcohol can cause stomach ulcers, kidney damage and fatal disease of the liver. Heavy drinkers are 10 times more likely to die from cirrhosis of the liver than non-drinkers. Alcohol is thought to be the major contributory factor to 35,000 premature deaths each year.

A *Why do you think that drinking alcohol is so attractive to both the young and the old?*

Alcoholism

We need to understand the meaning of the following two terms:

1 A 'heavy drinker' is someone who frequently resorts to drinking alcohol, increases his or her consumption of alcohol noticeably over a short period of time and is often incapable of thinking clearly.

2 An 'alcoholic' is a person who has become totally reliant on their daily intake of alcohol. Their body needs this to such an extent that if alcohol is withheld, it suffers marked 'withdrawal symptoms'.

It is thought that well over 2,000,000 people in the U.K. are heavily dependent on alcohol with some 900,000 being confirmed alcoholics. Why, though, do people follow this path?

a) *Personal and psychological pressures.* In the beginning a sense of loneliness, inadequacy or anxiety may lead to a dependence on alcohol.

b) *Social pressures.* Most drinking takes place in a social environment although the heavy drinker will also drink privately. That is a danger sign.

c) *Unemployment.* Tests have shown that people who are unemployed are more likely to drink heavily, even though they have less spare money to spend on alcohol.

d) *Advertising.* Some £2,500,000 is spent each year by the drinks industry on advertising within the U.K. This has been a major factor in increasing alcohol consumption by over 100% in the last 40 years.

B *How influential do you think advertisements are in persuading people to drink? What about young people in particular?*

Help?

Alcohol can lead to the same level of dependency and addiction as other forms of drugs. People who are addicted need the help of others and that is where Alcoholics Anonymous plays a leading role. Started in the U.S.A. in the 1930s, this organisation exists to help those people who are seriously addicted while Al-Anon, a sister organisation, seeks to help the families of alcoholics.

C *Alcohol is now readily available at almost any hour. What effect do you think this has had on the drinking habits of people?*

ANSWER IN YOUR BOOK …

1 What is a 'heavy drinker' and what is an 'alcoholic'?

2 What are the main effects of heavy drinking and alcoholism?

3 Why do you think that men are much more likely to be affected by alcohol-related problems than women?

FIND OUT AND NOTE …

Alcoholics Anonymous, formed in the 1930s, is the most well-known organisation offering help to the heavy drinker and the alcoholic. Discover as much as you can about the way it works. In particular, find out the following:

a) The AA's 12 point programme of recovery and the part that 'God' plays in the programme.

b) The way that 'recovered alcoholics' are expected to play their part in supporting those struggling with their addiction.

READ AND DECIDE …

The Bible appears to support a 'moderate drinking' approach by Christians. St Paul, however, made an interesting suggestion which could cover the drinking of alcohol as well as other activities. He wrote:
"I am free to do anything, you say. Yes, but not everything does good. No doubt I am free to do anything, but I for one will not let anything make free with me." (1.Corinthians 6.12)

❖ Make out a case for a Christian to abstain from alcohol because of the effect that it has upon other people and on society in general.

IN THE GLOSSARY …

Old Testament; Alcoholic.

5.6 GAMBLING

Heavy gambling, in which large sums of money are regularly won and lost, is an addiction just like alcoholism and drug-taking. Gamblers Anonymous, which was set up to help gamblers and their families, estimates that over 100,000 people are addicted to gambling in the U.K. alone.

Why do people gamble?

The statistics about gambling are quite revealing:

1 40% of the adult population in the U.K. gambles regularly.

2 Men are twice as likely as women to be regular gamblers.

3 35% of the U.K. population fill in football pools. In the opening week of the National Lottery, over 30,000,000 tickets were sold with one in two of the U.K. population thought to have bought at least one.

4 Gambling among young people has increased rapidly in recent years. Most schools in large towns and cities now consider themselves to have a 'gambling problem', with special events being laid on at lunchtimes in some schools to keep the pupils on the premises.

What is the great attraction of gambling?

a) It feeds the illusions that many people have of growing wealthy. The prizes in the football pools and the National Lottery in the U.K. have been carefully set to offer everyone the chance of becoming an 'instant millionaire'. Gamblers Anonymous points out that all of us secretly want to become powerful. Money brings power.

b) It works upon our reasoning that we can't lose all the time and that if we keep trying we will eventually beat the system. Few people take the odds against winning seriously into account. The first National Lottery in the U.K. offered each person odds of 14,000,000 to 1 against winning the jackpot but that did not stop everyone dreaming!

c) It is an antidote to the everyday boredom and loneliness that characterise so many lives. Young people want instant excitement, hence the popularity of the fruit machines which pay out as soon as the win is registered. As soon as most of us win, of course, the money goes straight back in!

d) It is an answer to the insecurity that many of us feel about the future. Most of us feel that a large win would change our whole lives for the better. Experience should teach us that this is not always the case. The mass media is full of examples of people whose lives have fallen apart after a sudden and unexpected influx of money. You might like to reflect on why this is.

A Do you think that access to gambling should be so easy?

Gambling – the cost

Like any other form of 'addiction', the compulsive gambler begins to need more and more of the 'drug' – in this case the excitement and power that gambling brings. If they do win, a large part of their winnings will be used to finance more gambling. If they lose they will beg, steal or borrow to recoup their losses. Either way, the outcome is invariably disastrous. Gambling often causes tensions within relationships, destroys businesses and in some cases can ultimately lead to suicide.

Some Christians are strongly opposed to gambling while others take a more lenient view. All, however, are very concerned about the unhappiness that gambling causes, both to the gambler and the rest of his/her family. They point out that the Bible condemns the attitude which lies at the heart of gambling – the love of money. You can read what St Paul had to say about that in 1.Timothy 6.9,10.

B *The National Lottery has been an enormous success. Can you explain why?*

READ AND DECIDE ...

St Paul had some very strong words to say about the love of money. Read them through carefully:
  "Those who want to be rich fall into temptations and snares and into many foolish and harmful desires which plunge people into ruin and destruction. The love of money is the root of all evil, and in pursuit of it ... some have spiked themselves on many a painful thorn." (1.Timothy 6.9,10)

a) Do you agree that the 'love of money' is at the very root of gambling?

b) What do you think might be some of the 'temptations', 'snares', and 'foolish and harmful desires' which await those people who want to be rich?

c) Do you think that gambling falls under this overall condemnation by St Paul? Are there any other modern activities which, you think, might be similarly condemned?

ANSWER IN YOUR BOOK ...

1 Can you explain why so many people gamble?

2 Who do you think are the most vulnerable groups in society to gambling? Can you try to explain why?

3 Can you explain the great attraction of gambling to young people?

CAN YOU EXPLAIN?

It is a fact that far more men gamble than women. Can you explain why?

6 PREJUDICE AND DISCRIMINATION

6.1 RACISM

When we talk about 'racism' there are four words which are central to the debate. A careful definition of each one of them is essential:

1 *Racism.* This is a belief in the superiority of one race over all others. The superiority may be physical, intellectual or spiritual. If such a belief is strongly held, it can have an immense influence over the way that one group of people treats another.

2 *Prejudice.* Prejudice is an attitude of mind which allows someone to 'prejudge' others from a different racial group. It is a short step from believing one racial group to be inferior to treating them as such. What we believe has a great effect on our actions.

3 *Stereotyping.* Prejudice and stereotyping are closely related. Stereotyping takes place when all members of a certain group are thought to share the same characteristics. These stereotypes are then

used as the basis for racial abuse – i.e: "All ...... are lazy"; "everyone from ...... smells of ......" or "all ...... are thick".

4 *Discrimination.* If prejudice is in the mind then discrimination takes place in the real world. Discrimination happens when people are unfairly treated because of their racial origins. Many countries, including Britain, have passed laws to try to ensure that all their citizens are treated fairly in such important areas as housing, education and employment. However, these laws are notoriously difficult to apply. How do you prove, for example, that someone has been passed over for a job because of the colour of their skin?

A *A mixed marriage. Why do you think that some people see mixed marriages as real threats to their way of life in the U.K? Do you agree?*

What causes racism?

Until comparatively recently geographical barriers, such as oceans, mountain ranges and deserts, kept the different races apart. This allowed each group of people to develop their own national and racial characteristics – size and build; physical features and colour.

This isolation allowed an attitude to set in which is still with us today and forms the foundation of much racism. Like almost every other animal, human beings feel safest when they are surrounded by their own kind. 'Outsiders' are usually met with a mixture of suspicion and fear. Such fear, fuelled by ignorance, is at the root of much racial hatred. It often lies dormant in a society and within individuals for a long time. Then an

incident sparks it off and it comes to the surface. Racism can take one of two forms:

a) It can be directed by individuals against other people. Racial attacks on immigrants, for instance, are still common-place in Britain in those areas where there is a high immigrant population.

b) It can be institutionalised. There have been many examples of this during the past century. To mention just two:
   ❖ In Germany during the 1930s, the Nazis created much hatred against the Jews. They were then able to eliminate six million Jews with virtually no opposition.
   ❖ Between 1948 and 1994 a system of apartheid was kept in place in South Africa. This system denied almost every human right to the country's black and coloured populations. You will find out more about this form of racism in Unit 6.3.

> **B** *Racial prejudice is not a problem at this age. How do you think some people grow up to be racially prejudiced? Why does it affect some people and not others?*

IN YOUR OWN WORDS ...

a) In this unit you have been introduced to four important terms. Explain each of them in your own words:
   ❖ Racism
   ❖ Racial Prejudice
   ❖ Racial discrimination
   ❖ Stereotyping

   During the next week watch out on TV and in newspapers for any incidents in which some form of racism was involved. Try to work out, and explain, the causes of the conflict in each case.

b) Do you think that racism is a problem in the U.K. today? What more do you think we could do to overcome it?

ANSWER IN YOUR BOOK ...

1 What is prejudice and how does it often lead to discrimination?

2 Why did racial prejudice and discrimination take a very long time to develop?

3 How can racism express itself?

IN THE GLOSSARY ...

Immigrant; Racial Prejudice; Racial Discrimination; Stereotyping.

6.2 THE BLACK COMMUNITY IN BRITAIN

People have been coming to settle in Britain for many centuries. Viking, Roman and Norman invaders all intermarried with the early inhabitants of these islands. They have left their imprint on the language, landscape, way of life and 'national characteristics' of Britain.

Over the centuries, immigrants have come to live in Britain for two main reasons:

a) *To work*. In the 19th century, many Irishmen came to Britain to work in the construction industry building railways, roads and houses. Then, in the 1950s and the 1960s, the British Government encouraged people from the Caribbean, India and Pakistan to live and work in Britain. They were brought here because the Second World War had robbed this country of many male workers. Thousands came and most of them ended up doing the work that no one else was prepared to tackle.

b) *To escape persecution in their home country*. It was for this reason that;
   ❖ many Jews and Poles fled to Britain before and after the Second World War;
   ❖ in the 1970s, Asians who fled from Uganda found refuge in Britain;
   ❖ 'boat people' from Vietnam and Kurds from Turkey came to Britain during the 1970s and 1980s.

Many of these immigrants found it very difficult to find accommodation so they settled in the poorer areas of cities such as Manchester, Birmingham and London. As friends and relatives arrived, they went to the same areas and ethnic communities began to form. Today there are about 2,500,000 coloured people in Britain, some 4% of the total population. Tougher leglislation has now been introduced to severely limit the number of immigrants allowed to settle in Britain.

The Law and Race Relations

Ever since immigration started in earnest, black people in Britain have faced abuse, harassment and violence. In 1976 the Race Relations Act became law and this attempted to protect every citizen in the U.K. from racial discrimination. It offered to every black person

A *What practical steps do you think could be taken to improve relations between black and white people in Britain?*

exactly the same rights as a white person applying for a job; trying to rent accommodation; buying something from a shop or working for an employer. The Race Relations Act also made 'incitement to racial hatred' an offence.

The Race Relations Act represented a major step forward in improving the lot of black people in Britain. Yet it seems to have made little impact on changing the attitudes of people. A Social Attitudes Survey, carried out in 1985, found that:

1 35% of white people interviewed were prepared to describe themselves as racially prejudiced. One wonders how many more were not prepared to admit it?
2 66% of black people in the survey felt sure that they had been denied a job at some time or other because of the colour of their skin.

Do you think these statistics are surprising?

Christians and Race

Christians are committed to the belief that all people, black and white, are equal in the sight of God. No race can be the intellectual, physical or spiritual superior of another. Everyone has been created by God and so must be equal. Distinctions based on colour, class or sex do not apply. That is the clear teaching of Paul in Galatians 3.28.

The Christian Church, however, has often failed to put this ideal into action:

a) Christian missionaries have persecuted and killed other races in the name of their faith. In the 16th century, for instance, Roman Catholic Spanish conquistadors invaded South America and put to death those people who would not convert to Christianity.

b) Apartheid in South Africa was actively supported by the white Dutch Reformed Church.

c) When black immigrants from the Caribbean came to Britain in the 1950s and 1960s they were not given a warm welcome by the churches. Instead, they set up their own churches which have since flourished.

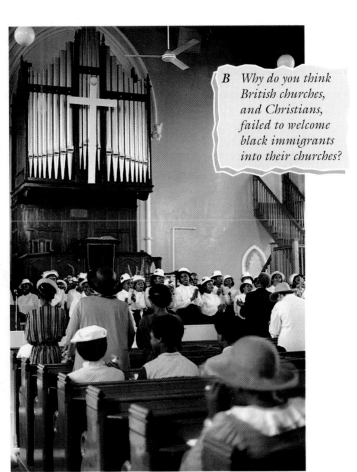

B Why do you think British churches, and Christians, failed to welcome black immigrants into their churches?

ANSWER IN YOUR BOOK ...

1 Why have many immigrants come to live in Britain in the 20th century?

2 How have ethnic communities emerged within many British cities?

3 What was the Race Relations Act of 1976 and what did it try to achieve?

WHAT DO YOU THINK?

a) Why do you think that racial hatred and harassment is almost always directed towards immigrants who are not white? Why is it not directed towards white people as well?

b) Why do you think that the Race Relations Act has failed to influence people's thinking about race?

c) Why do you think that many people are willing to flout the law and continue to discriminate against black people?

FIND OUT AND NOTE ...

Although legislation is now in place to outlaw racial discrimination, few people doubt that it still exists in Britain. Try to find out about the following:

a) Any examples from the television or newspapers where black people have been stereotyped.

b) Any examples from the Mass Media showing discrimination against black people in the areas of housing, employment or education.

c) Any attacks on black people which have been racially motivated.

d) Any claims about people in the public services being racially motivated in their actions.

e) Any examples of racial harassment.

IN THE GLOSSARY ...

Immigrant; Racial Discrimination; Racial Prejudice; Missionary; Apartheid.

6.3 APARTHEID

The most notorious example of racial discrimination in the modern world was the policy of 'apartheid'. It was put in place in South Africa in 1948 and finally dismantled in 1994. Apartheid was officially described as the 'separate development of blacks and whites'.

The racial breakdown of the population of South Africa is drawn from four distinct ethnic groups:

1 African blacks. (74%)
2 Whites. (15%)
3 Coloureds/Mixed Race. (8%)
4 Indians/Asians. (3%)

Apartheid

European settlers moved into South Africa in the early part of the 19th century and dominated the native black population. They took over huge areas of land and employed black people, on very low wages, to work mainly in the mines and other forms of industry and agriculture. The white population exported huge quantities of diamonds, coal, gold, fruit and wine and grew rich on the proceeds. They denied any part of this wealth to the black majority. By the 1980s, 87% of the land in South Africa was in white hands even though only 15% of the overall population were white.

In 1948 the South African government officially established the policy of apartheid. This reinforced the gulf which already existed between the white, privileged minority and the black, poor majority. In the years that followed laws were passed which:

a) excluded blacks from the best cinemas, buses, schools and hospitals. These were designated 'whites only';
b) allowed local councils to designate park benches, beaches and other social amenities for the use of whites only;
c) outlawed marriage and any sexual relations between black and white people. Until 1985 it was illegal for whites and non-whites to mix socially, with all non-whites having to carry an identity pass;
d) confined blacks to 'homelands' in certain parts of the country where the housing, schools, public transport and other facilities were appalling.

Between 1960 and 1984 some 3,500,000 blacks

A *This photograph shows a traditional South African homeland from the early 1980s. What do you think the white South African government hoped to gain by treating the blacks in this way?*

were forcibly moved out of their homes into these homelands or Bantustans, as they were called. Some were forced out because whites claimed their land while others were evicted when their labour was no longer needed locally. The government argued that the blacks were returning to their traditional homelands. By the time that the policy was abandoned about 40% of all blacks lived on the homelands.

Nelson Mandela was an opponent of apartheid who spent 26 years in prison for his opposition to the system. He was released by the South African President, F.W. De Klerk, in 1990 and moves were taken swiftly to end apartheid. All South Africans were given the right to vote for the first time and free elections were held in 1994. Nelson Mandela was elected President by a large majority but the work of providing for the needs of all South Africans had only just begun. It will be many years before the housing, schools and employment opportunities of black people in South Africa can be brought up to the same standards as those of the white population.

ANSWER IN YOUR BOOK ...

1 What is apartheid?
2 Why was apartheid introduced in South Africa?
3 What were the main consequences of apartheid for the black population in South Africa?

READ AND DECIDE ...

The World Council of Churches is an umbrella organisation linking together most of the world's Churches. Since its formation in 1948 it has strongly opposed racism in all forms. It had this to say in one of its statements in 1980:

"Every human being created in the image of God is a person for whom Christ died. Racism, which is the use of a person's racial origin to determine a person's value, is an assault on Christ's values, and a rejection of his sacrifice."

a) Read Genesis chapters 1 and 2 and then try to explain what it means to say that men and women are created in the image of God.

b) With John 3.16 in mind, can you explain how Christ died for all human beings?

c) How does Paul argue, in Galatians 3.26-28, that all human beings belong to the same family?

d) Who, according to Matthew 25.31-45, suffers when people reject the stranger and those in need?

IN YOUR OWN WORDS ...

Look up and make notes on each of the three following references:

a) Leviticus 19.33-34
b) Numbers 15.15
c) Acts 10.34,35

What do you think is the relevance of these verses to any discussion on apartheid or racial discrimination?

IN THE GLOSSARY ...

Racial Discrimination; Apartheid.

6.4 NON-VIOLENT PROTEST

If you watch children squabbling in the playground, or adults on the football pitch, it is easy to see how quickly a minor dispute can explode into anger and violence. Often, in different parts of the world, people have protested peacefully against some aspect of their government's policy only to find themselves confronted with violence. Here are two examples:

a) At Sharpeville, a black township in South Africa, a peaceful protest by children and young people in March 1960 was met with violence from the authorities. Many were killed in the incident.

b) A rally of students in Tianamen Square, China, in May 1989 ended in tragedy as many were killed by Army tanks.

In this century two outstanding figures have denounced violence in all forms. They have spoken out for a form of non-violent protest – passive resistance. They were Mahatma Gandhi in India and Martin Luther King in the U.S.A. Both men put their ideas into action and both, sadly, met violent deaths.

Mahatma Gandhi (1869-1948)

Born in India Mahatma Gandhi, a Hindu, spent much of his early life in South Africa. He was outraged by the injustices of the system that he found there. This was in the time well before apartheid was officially introduced. When Gandhi returned home to India it was to a country occupied and governed by the British.

Gandhi taught the people that they should be free to govern themselves since that was a basic human right. At the same time it would be immoral and impractical to attempt to remove the British by force. Instead, he developed a very effective policy of non-cooperation and non-violent protest. He organised large unarmed protest marches as well as going on a hunger strike himself. The British Army had no answer to this policy. In 1947 the British left India, which soon became an independent country. Only a year later, however, Gandhi was assassinated.

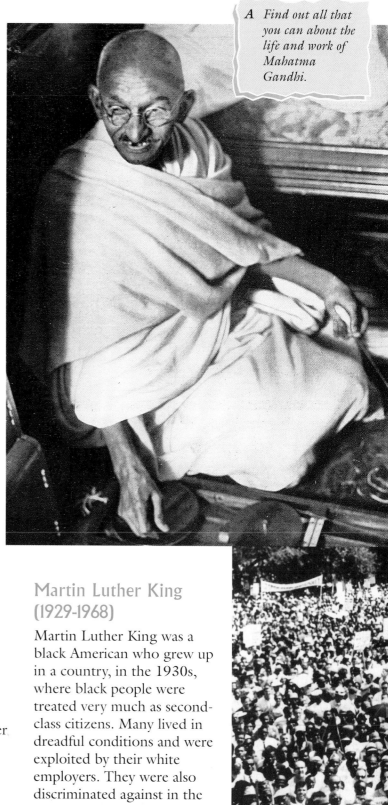

A *Find out all that you can about the life and work of Mahatma Gandhi.*

Martin Luther King (1929-1968)

Martin Luther King was a black American who grew up in a country, in the 1930s, where black people were treated very much as second-class citizens. Many lived in dreadful conditions and were exploited by their white employers. They were also discriminated against in the areas of public transport, employment and shopping.

In the 1950s and 1960s black people began to find their voice and protest against such injustices. There were riots in several cities which had large black populations. Things were in grave danger of getting out of hand when the Reverend Martin Luther King began to teach his fellow blacks that there was another way. He organised:

❖ 'bus boycotts'. Black people refused to use public buses unless they were desegregated (black and white people allowed to sit side by side). In 1956, a law was passed making racial segregation on America's buses illegal;

❖ boycotts of cafés, restaurants and schools which followed policies of segregation (separate seats and areas for blacks and whites);

❖ 'freedom marches' across America. In 1960 he led one such march on Washington where 250,000 demonstrators demanded that black people be given the right to vote. On these marches black and white people marched together.

In April, 1968 Martin Luther King was shot dead by a white man while he was in a hotel in Memphis, Tennessee. He was just 39 years old.

B Find out all that you can about the life and teachings of Martin Luther King.

ANSWER IN YOUR BOOK ...

1 What is 'passive resistance'?
2 How did Gandhi develop non-violent protest in India?
3 How did Martin Luther King fight discrimination in the U.S.A?

FIND OUT AND NOTE ...

By now you should have discovered a great deal about both Mahatma Gandhi and Martin Luther King. Write an article for a magazine of between 500 and 600 words on one of them underlining, in particular, their teachings and indicating why you think they were so effective.

IN YOUR OWN WORDS ...

Martin Luther King was a great orator and preacher. His most famous speech began with the words 'I have a dream...'. Can you find out something about this speech and then summarise it in your own words.

WHAT DO YOU THINK?

Here are two quotations. Read them through carefully:

a) **Mahatma Gandhi:**
"In non-violence the masses have a weapon which enables a child, a woman, or even a decrepit old man to resist the mightiest government successfully."

b **Martin Luther King:**
"To resist without bitterness,
To be cursed and not reply
To be beaten and not hit back
Is at the heart of the Creed of non-violence."

Now read what Paul had to say in Romans 13.1,2. Do you think that non-violent opposition is a Christian way of opposing unjust Government policies? If so, can this be reconciled with the words of Paul?

IN THE GLOSSARY ...

Apartheid; Segregation.

6.5 VIOLENT PROTEST

There is a very strong pacifist tradition in Protestant Christianity. We have seen in Unit 6.4 how Martin Luther King, taking his lead from Mahatma Gandhi, applied the principle of non-violent protest to the struggle of black people in the U.S.A. A similar approach was encouraged by Bishop Desmond Tutu as the blacks in South Africa suffered under the policy of apartheid (see Unit 6.3). The inspiration for both of these reformers came from the teachings of Jesus in the New Testament.

Others have read the New Testament and come to very different conclusions. During the 1960s and 1970s, for instance, many countries in Latin America were ruled by military dictatorships. All forms of human rights were denied and any attempt at non-violent protest was ruthlessly suppressed.

Two priests from this era believed that God had called them to play an active role in overthrowing their governments – to meet force with force:

1   *Ernesto Cardinale*. The regime of the corrupt dictator, Samoza, in Nicaragua during the 1960s was brutal. Ernesto Cardinale, a Roman Catholic priest and poet, played a leading part in the guerrilla war which led to the overthrow of Samoza. He argued that:
❖ the Nicaraguan government of Samoza had declared war on the people by its corrupt legal system, brutal beatings, torture and mass killings. It was a situation that the people should no longer be expected to tolerate;
❖ as a Catholic priest, the claims of the Gospel on him demanded that he identify himself totally with the poor of Nicaragua. Jesus himself had declared that the poor and dispossessed would enter God's Kingdom ahead of the rich and powerful and Cardinale argued that the Church could only be true to the Christian Gospel if it did the same. The only way that the oppression could be lifted was by using arms.

A *Imagine yourself to have been a priest in Nicaragua in the 1970s. What would you have done in this situation?*

B *Can you find out a little more about the work and ideas of Camilo Torres?*

2 *Camilo Torres*. Camilo Torres became a priest in Colombia in the 1950s and was immediately horrified by the way that the poor peasants of the country were treated. He realised that a revolution was necessary since the rich would not give up their wealth voluntarily. His vision was of a Christian revolution in which the 'values' of oppression were replaced by those which come from the Gospels. This upset the Roman Catholic Church authorities and he was given the choice of stopping his work among the poor or leaving the priesthood. He gave up being a priest although the peasants continued to treat him as one. He joined one of the guerrilla movements in the mountainous regions of Colombia and was killed, in a battle, in 1966. Two years later a large number of Colombian priests signed a declaration which called for a revolution to be launched against corrupt government. They also called for the setting up of a government which took the problems of the people seriously and begin the long process of building a fair and equal society in the country.

Torres and Cardinale were two of the earliest representatives of a movement which was to have a considerable impact in both Latin America and elsewhere. It is called 'Liberation Theology'. This approach to Christianity believes that the Church must always place itself on the side of the poor, whatever the consequences might be. It teaches that the stories in the Gospel must be read in the light of the peoples' actual situation.

ANSWER IN YOUR BOOK ...

1 What was the situation in Latin America which gave rise to the work of Ernesto Cardinale and Camilo Torres?

2 How did Ernesto Cardinale justify his belief that the use of force was necessary in Nicaragua?

3 What is Liberation Theology?

READ AND DECIDE ...

Here are two quotations for you to think about:

❖ **Luke 4.18:**
"The Spirit of the Lord is upon me
because he has anointed me;
he has sent me to announce good news to the poor,
to proclaim release for prisoners
and recovery of sight for the blind;
to let the broken victims go free..."

❖ **Camilo Torres:**
"revolution is necessary to free the hungry, give drink to the thirsty, clothe the naked, and procure a life of well-being for the needy majority of the people."

Compare both of these extracts with the words of Jesus in Matthew 25.31-46.

a) Do you think that these two quotations are saying exactly the same thing?

b) What was the major difference between the ministry of Jesus and that of Camilo Torres?

c) If Jesus had been born into 20th century Nicaragua, what do you think his reaction would have been to the poverty, need and brutal treatment of the people?

IN THE GLOSSARY ...

Apartheid; Gospels; Liberation Theology.

6.6 ANTI-SEMITISM

Nearly all of the early followers of Jesus were Jews and for some time, Christianity was little more than an off-shoot of the Jewish religion. It was not long, however, before tension arose between the old, traditional faith of the Jews and the new beliefs of the Christians. Traces of this tension can be found in the New Testament in the Gospels and the letters of Paul. For three centuries, however, the Jews and the Christians had one thing in common – they were both persecuted by the Romans.

Then, in 312 CE, the Roman Emperor Constantine 'converted' to Christianity. This ushered in a time when the Christians were spared any further persecution. The Roman anger was directed against the Jews and the Christian Church lent its enthusiastic support. Christian leaders could see nothing good in the Jewish faith. Had it not, after all, brought about the death of God's Son, Jesus?

The growth of anti-semitism

From the 6th century, Jews began to come to Britain to live although the major influx did not take place until William the Conqueror invaded in 1066. The Jewish immigrants settled in the largest towns and, before long, became very successful merchants and money-lenders. They tried to draw as little attention to themselves as possible because they were aware of the hatred that some people had for the Jews.

Around the times of the Crusades (11th and 12th centuries) Christian fanatics executed many Jews in York, Norwich and London. A dreadful massacre, for example, took place in York in 1190 when a Christian mob burnt a large number of Jews to death in a tower. A century later all Jews were expelled from Britain and were not allowed back until 1650.

In the centuries that followed the Roman Catholic Church held several Councils to discuss the Jews and two charges were regularly made against them:

a) That they were responsible for the death of God's Son, Jesus Christ.
b) That they murdered Christian children and used their blood for their own religious worship. This charge, first made in Norwich in 1154, became known as the 'blood libel'.

In the 16th century anti-semitism (hatred directed specifically against the Jews) was widespread throughout Europe. The 16th century Protestant reformer, Martin Luther, wrote several books and pamphlets directed against the Jews, encouraging Christians to burn down their synagogues and show no mercy to them at all. This, of course, is just what Adolf Hitler did in the 1930s (see Unit 6.7). The Nazis indoctrinated the people against the Jews; humiliated Jewish children in schools; arranged boycotts of shops owned by Jewish people; burnt Jewish synagogues to the ground; arrested Jewish people; paraded them in public and herded them into ghetto's. Later, Jews were arrested and sent to concentration camps where 6,000,000 were killed. Their only 'crime' was that of being Jewish. This was the supreme example of

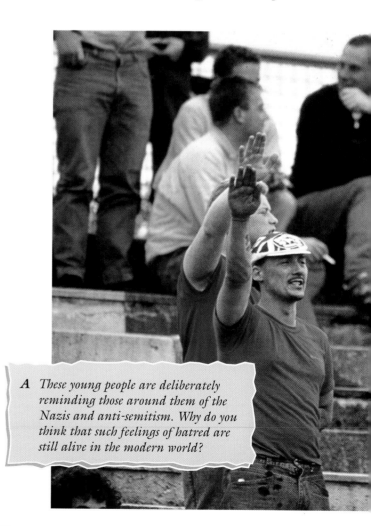

A *These young people are deliberately reminding those around them of the Nazis and anti-semitism. Why do you think that such feelings of hatred are still alive in the modern world?*

anti-semitism, although homosexuals and gypsies also suffered in a similar way in Nazi Germany.

Unfortunately, anti-semitism is still a problem today. In the U.K.

B With Matthew 27.20-26 open in front of you, can you explain the main charge which Christians levelled against the Jews for centuries?

Jewish graves are still vandalised from time to time and Jewish families are threatened by neo-Nazi, right-wing fascist groups such as the National Front. Recent events in the old East Germany and other European countries have demonstrated that the anti-Jewish hatred which spilled over during the Holocaust is still alive.

ANSWER IN YOUR BOOK ...

1 What is anti-semitism?

2 In what ways has anti-semitism shown itself in the U.K? Why did it start?

3 What are the main charges which were levelled by the Christians against the Jews?

DISCUSS AMONG YOURSELVES...

a) Why do you think that the Jews have, in the past, been singled out as a group to be hated and reviled?

b) Can you think of any other group in society which has been persecuted in a similar way to the Jews?

c) Can you think of three reasons why Christians, and others, have persecuted the Jews in the past?

d) Collect together as many examples as you can to show that anti-semitism still prospers at home and abroad, using radio, television, newspapers and magazines for your source material. You will need to allocate several weeks, off and on, to this exercise. Then write up your notes before writing an essay of some 500 words with the title: 'Anti-semitism throughout history'.

FIND OUT AND NOTE ...

Carry out some research of your own into the activities of the Fascists in England during the 1930s. In particular, try to discover the following:

a) Why did they object so strongly to the Jewish presence in England?

b) Could such an organisation exist today? Give reasons for your answer.

IN THE GLOSSARY ...

Anti-semitism; New Testament; Gospels; Paul; Roman Catholic Church; Protestant; Synagogue; Holocaust.

6.7 THE HOLOCAUST

As a historical event, the Holocaust has no parallel. No group of people have suffered as the Jews did at the hands of the Nazis in the Second World War (1939-45). Centuries of anti-semitic hatred and fury exploded in the most frightening example of genocide. In just six years 6,000,000 (6 million) Jewish men, women and children met their deaths in concentration camps in Germany and Poland. They suffered and died not because they represented any threat to the authorities or the country but simply because they were Jews.

Death

The carnage of the German concentration camps was so horrific that people refer to those years in German history as the Holocaust. The word itself means a 'totally burnt offering'. Between 1935 and 1945 Jews throughout Nazi-occupied Europe were rounded up in vast numbers and shipped off by train to various concentration camps to be gassed.

There were 28 such concentration camps in all. Their names have become symbols in themselves – symbols of human degradation, inhumanity and death. Dachau, Buchenwald, Belsen and Treblinka all conjure up horrific pictures of emaciated men and women and piles of bones and skulls. Beyond these, however, one name stands supreme – Auschwitz. By 1944, 6,000 Jews were being gassed each day in Auschwitz.

Why did the Holocaust happen?

There were two main reasons:

a) The Nazis claimed that the Jews represented everything that threatened the future of the German race. Although many Jews occupied positions of importance in the political, social and business life of Germany, they were said to be uncommitted to Germany. Their main allegiance was said to be to God and the Jewish people.

b) The Jews, together with other minority groups in Germany such as gypsies and homosexuals, were seen as a threat to the 'racial purity' which Hitler was fervently trying to achieve in the German people.

A   In the days following the defeat of the Nazis in 1945, stories and pictures of scenes like this were broadcast around the world. What do you think its impact was upon ordinary men and women?

Responding to the Holocaust

It was only when the Second World War ended in 1945 that the whole world became fully aware of the horrors that had taken place. Although initially too shocked to make any response at all, the Jewish community soon committed itself to one task – that the world would never be allowed to forget what had happened in the Holocaust. The State of Israel was set up in 1947 as a statement of the belief that something good can arise out of horror and death.

Days of memorial were arranged, special prayers were written and places of remembrance were established to keep the memory of the Holocaust alive. Several concentration camps were left standing as silent witnesses to the atrocities that had taken place in them. A special Holocaust memorial was built, as the photograph shows, at Yad Vashem. Yad Vashem means 'a name and a place'. The place is a bare room lit by a single candle and the names are those of the various concentration camps written across the floor. There is also a line of trees at Yad Vashem called 'the Avenue of the Righteous', with a tree planted for every Gentile who helped a Jew during the war.

B *This stark memorial to the Holocaust was built in Yad Vashem in Israel. What do you think is its intended message to the world?*

ANSWER IN YOUR BOOK ...

1 What was the Holocaust?

2 Why did the Nazis set out to eliminate the entire Jewish race?

3 What is Yad Vashem?

WHAT DO YOU THINK?

Martin Niemoller, a German pastor during the Second World War, said the following:
    "In the Middle Ages Jews were told, You cannot live amongst us as Jews; in the modern age Jews were told, You cannot live amongst us; in the Nazi era Jews were told, You cannot live."

a) Carry out some research of your own into one other occasion, apart from the Holocaust, when the Jews were singled out and persecuted.

b) Why do you think that this particular group of people have been persecuted far more than any other?

DISCUSS AMONG YOURSELVES...

Dachau, in southern Germany, housed one of the worst of all the concentration camps. It is now a museum and this inscription can be found on one of its walls:

    PLUS JAMAIS
    NEVER AGAIN
    NIE WIEDER
    NIKOGDA BOLSHE

Can you think of three ways in which the rest of the world could make sure that an event as horrific as the Holocaust never happens again?

IN THE GLOSSARY ...

Holocaust; Anti-semitism; Homosexual; Gentile; Genocide.

7.1 ABORTION – THE FACTS

Before 1967 abortion (the ending of a pregnancy) was illegal in the U.K. However, a large number of 'back-street' abortions were carried out each year by totally unqualified people. Performed in horrific conditions, these illegal abortions sometimes resulted in death. Thousands of women were permanently harmed with life-long infertility a frequent result.

The Abortion Act

The Abortion Act (1967) was introduced in the U.K. to put an end to this once and for all. It made abortion legal in the following circumstances:

1 Two registered practitioners (doctors) had examined the woman and agreed that an abortion could be legally carried out.
2 The abortion had been carried out before 'the time of viability' i.e: the time when the baby could exist on its own outside its mother's womb. Medical opinion at the time put this 'time of viability' at 28 weeks of pregnancy but the Human Fertilisation and Embryology Act of 1990 lowered it to 24 weeks.
3 The continuation of the pregnancy would involve risk greater to the physical or mental health of the mother or any child within her family than if the pregnancy was terminated.
4 A termination was necessary to prevent permanent injury to the body or mind of the mother.
5 There was a real risk that the baby would be born mentally or physically handicapped.

Opponents of abortion say that the Act has created 'abortion on demand'. Supporters say that it simply faces up to the realities of the situation.

Abortion on demand?

It is a matter of opinion whether we have 'abortion on demand'. It is true to say, however, that few requests for a 'termination of pregnancy' cannot be performed under the Abortion Act in the U.K. Before reaching a conclusion about

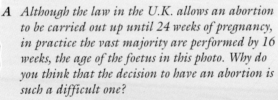

A   Although the law in the U.K. allows an abortion to be carried out up until 24 weeks of pregnancy, in practice the vast majority are performed by 16 weeks, the age of the foetus in this photo. Why do you think that the decision to have an abortion is such a difficult one?

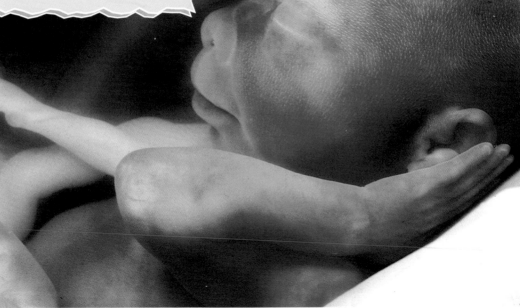

whether this is a good or bad thing, consider the following statistics:

a) Before 1967 an estimated 200,000 abortions were performed illegally each year in the U.K. About 60 women died annually as a result.

b) In 1986, 157,000 legal abortions were performed at the rate of some 300 a day in the U.K. By 1990, this figure had risen to 173,900. About 20% of these were carried out on women from other countries, especially Spain and southern Ireland where abortion is illegal.

c) Although the legal time limit on having an abortion is now 24 weeks they are rarely performed after 22 weeks, unless there are compelling medical reasons for doing so.

d) About 18% of all pregnancies (1 in 5) now end with an abortion.

What conclusions do you think can be drawn from these statistics?

B 44% of pregnancies now take place outside marriage. Is abortion the only answer to this social problem?

ANSWER IN YOUR BOOK ...

1 Why was it considered necessary to introduce the Abortion Act in the U.K. in 1967?

2 Under what circumstances can an abortion be legally performed in the U.K?

3 Is there any reason to think that abortion is now virtually available on demand in the U.K?

WHAT DO YOU THINK?

a) The law on abortion does not take the father's rights into consideration, even if he is married to the child's mother. Do you think that this is right?

b) The United Nations Declaration on Human Rights says:

"The child, by reason of his physical and mental immaturity, needs special safeguards and care, including appropriate legal protection, before as well as after birth."

Do you think that the Abortion Act goes against this principle?

USE YOUR IMAGINATION ...

Use your imagination to think of and describe the following:

a) Two situations in which a pregnancy would be very difficult to cope with, if not completely impossible.

b) Two situations in which a pregnancy would be very inconvenient and difficult to cope with.

c) Two situations in which a pregnancy would cause some inconvenience.

Explain what you think the mother and father should do in each situation.

IN THE GLOSSARY ...

Abortion.

Abortion is legal in the U.K. and in most Western countries. It remains, however, a highly controversial issue. In the U.S.A., for instance, opponents of abortion have resorted to burning down clinics and even murdering those held responsible for carrying out the operations. Abortion raises extremely strong emotions, both for and against.

For Abortion (Pro-Choice)

The arguments in support of abortion can be summarised as follows:

1 Women have the right to decide what happens to their own bodies and the foetus is part of that body. This is true up to the point when a baby can exist on its own outside its mother's womb. It is during this time that an abortion must be performed.

2 Every baby has the right to be born into a family which will be able to provide the basic necessities of life – shelter, food, clothing, etc. If this basic care cannot be offered then an abortion is justified.

3 There are too many unwanted babies in the world. Why add more?

4 Other members of the family have their own rights. This includes the mother's parents (if she is unmarried); her husband and any children she may already have.

5 If a woman discovers that her child is likely to be severally handicapped she must be allowed to decide whether she can look after the baby or not.

6 A woman who becomes pregnant after being raped should not, under any circumstances, be compelled to have the baby. Abortion is not always the easy option. Often it requires a sensible and mature decision. Almost certainly, there will be an emotional cost to be paid.

How powerful do you think these arguments are?

A *What do you think are the main arguments for abortion being allowed in our society?*

Against Abortion (Pro-Life)

The main arguments against legal abortion can be summarised as follows:

a) Every child is a precious and unique gift from God. We have no right to destroy that gift under any circumstances. This even includes the sad case of a woman being raped.

b) A defenceless baby needs special protection since it cannot stand up for its own rights. The rights of the unborn child are at least equal to those of the mother. Some would say they are even greater.

c) The embryo is a human being from the moment it is conceived. Left alone, it will develop into a person.

d) A baby who is physically or mentally handicapped can go on to lead a full and rewarding life.

e) Abortion places an overwhelming burden on doctors and nurses who are committed to saving life, not destroying it.

How strong do you think these arguments are?

Christians and abortion

The majority of Christians feel very unhappy about abortion and the increasing number of unwanted pregnancies. This has always been the case. The Didache, the oldest surviving Christian document written in about 70 CE, stated:

"You shall not kill by abortion the fruit of the womb and you shall not murder the infant already born."

Most Churches are equally strong in their condemnation of abortion. In 1984 the Church of England said that the unborn foetus should be protected. It might, though, have to be sacrificed if the life of the mother was threatened. To the Roman Catholic Church, the deliberate ending of a pregnancy is a sin in all circumstances. (Refer to **FIND OUT AND NOTE...**)

B What is the main thrust of this Pro-life poster?

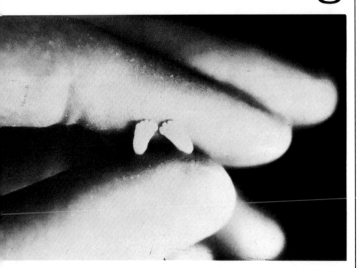

These feet were made for walking

an adult holds the feet of an aborted baby of about 11 weeks

Life
CAMPAIGNS
LIFE House,
Newbold Terrace,
LEAMINGTON SPA.
Warwickshire CV32 4EA
0926 421587

ANSWER IN YOUR BOOK ...

1 What are the main arguments in favour of abortion?
2 What are the main arguments against abortion?
3 What is the general opinion among the Christian Churches about abortion?

WHAT DO YOU THINK?

There are many contentious points made in the text from both sides of the argument on abortion. Each of them is well worth thinking about and discussing.

a) The crucial issue is the question of whether an embryo is a human being from the moment it is conceived or whether a foetus only becomes a human being when it can survive on its own outside the mother's womb. What do you think?

b) The Roman Catholic Church maintains that it is wrong to destroy life at any time. Even a woman who has been raped or is expecting a handicapped baby cannot have an abortion. What do you think?

c) The Roman Catholic Church believes that the rights of an unborn baby are at least equal to, if not greater than, the rights of the mother. What do you think?

FIND OUT AND NOTE ...

The Roman Catholic condemns abortion more strongly than any other Church. Here are two examples. Read them carefully.

a) **The Second Vatican Council, 1963:**
"Life must be protected with the utmost care from the moment of conception: abortion and infanticide are abominable crimes."

b) **Pope Paul VI. Humanae Vitae, 1968:**
"Human life is sacred. All men must recognise this fact."

Can you find out exactly why the Roman Catholic Church condemns abortion so strongly? These quotations will offer you one or two clues.

IN THE GLOSSARY ...

Abortion; Foetus; Embryo.

During the early 1980s a new and terrifying disease hit the headlines – AIDS (Acquired Immune Deficiency Syndrome). In 1987 the British Government sent an information leaflet about AIDS to every family in Britain. The leaflet said:

> "Any man or woman can get the AIDS virus depending on their behaviour. It is not just a homosexual disease. There is no cure and it kills. By the time you have read this probably 300 people will have died in this country. It is believed that a further 30,000 carry the virus. The number is rising and will continue to rise unless we all take precautions."

A *Do you think that the fear of catching AIDS is likely to have a lasting effect on people's sexual behaviour?*

What is AIDS?

AIDS is caused by a virus – the Human Immuno-deficiency Virus (HIV). If the virus enters the bloodstream it attacks the cells which maintain the body's natural defence mechanisms. Once inside a cell the virus multiplies until it eventually destroys the cell. The person's defence mechanism begins to fail until they are unable to recover from infections which would not normally kill them.

This process may take years. No one knows why the HIV virus suddenly becomes active after years in the body and some people who become infected with HIV do not go on to develop full-blown AIDS.

Who catches AIDS – and how?

Throughout the 1980s and into the 1990s millions of people worldwide have contracted AIDS. The numbers

Get this straight: it's an HIV test or no mortgage

Patients of Aids-victim dentist 'at slight risk'

Inquiry launched into Aids claims
Tokyo court ponders as Aids case plaintiffs die

Man 'stabbed to death woman he thought had given him Aids'

HIV surgeon may be disciplined

Son dying of Aids revealed family's murderous secret

Missionary nurse who caught Aids through caring

Research success lifts Aids gloom

Aids girl's parents sue

Aids deaths in Italy

£4 saliva kit means more people will face HIV test

Duchess tested twice for HIV

Actor's wife dies of Aids

The war against Aids at home and in the lab

Women sue over Aids

continue to increase rapidly . The groups of people most at risk are:

1 homosexual and bisexual men;
2 drug users who share needles among themselves;
3 haemophiliacs and others who receive unscreened blood.

Obviously, the sexual partners of these people and, sadly, babies born to infected mothers, also run a heavy risk. To begin with AIDS was called 'the gay plague' because the people first affected in the U.K. were almost all homosexuals. Very soon, however, it became apparent that AIDS in other countries was more likely to affect heterosexuals. About 1 in 4 people now affected with AIDS in Britain contract it through having unprotected heterosexual sex.

Blood in the U.K. is now screened and safe. Apart from sharing infected needles, therefore, the only way that someone is going to contract AIDS is by having unprotected sex. HIV is a risk when body fluids such as

B   Imagine that this group of young people are discussing AIDS. With AIDS in mind, what advice would you give them as far as their own sexual behaviour is concerned?

semen, vaginal juices and blood are exchanged between one person and another. The risks are highest in certain forms of sexual activity:

1 *Anal intercourse.* This occurs when the penis enters the anus or bottom. It carries an extremely high risk because some form of bleeding is very likely.

2 *Unprotected vaginal intercourse.* The virus can be passed on by both men and women in this way if they do not take precautions by using a condom.

3 *Oral sex.* When a person stimulates the sexual organs of the other person with their tongue the virus can pass from one to the other, at least in theory. In practice, however, it is very unlikely to happen.

The condom is not only a highly efficient form of contraception in its own right but it also offers real protection against transmitting sexual diseases – including AIDS.

ANSWER IN YOUR BOOK ...

1 What is the HIV virus and how is it caught?
2 What is the link between the HIV virus and AIDS?
3 How is HIV caught?

WHAT DO YOU THINK?

Here are four statements made by young people about AIDS. Each of them raise important issues not only about AIDS but also our whole attitude to sexual activity. Try to work out what these issues are.

a) "The only complete answer to the problem of AIDS lies in the old Christian virtues of chastity outside marriage and total faithfulness within it." *Alan, 19.*

b) "When a person enters into a new sexual relationship he or she must be completely honest about their sexual history. Otherwise, they could be guilty of signing the other person's death warrant." *Anne, 21.*

c) "In the age of AIDS no-one in their right mind would go in for sleeping around" *Gill, 18.*

d) "AIDS is essentially different from all other sexual diseases. It will force us to re-examine our attitude to sex, and other issues, like nothing else has done." *Phil, 19.*

WRITE AN ESSAY ...

Carry out some research of your own before writing about 500 words on the title:
'The AIDS epidemic and the dangers it represents.'

IN THE GLOSSARY ...

Homosexual; Bisexuals; Heterosexual; Condom; Contraception.

When the HIV epidemic hit the headlines in the early 1980s it caused panic and terror in many quarters. To begin with it appeared that only homosexuals were being infected and this led to a widespread outbreak of homophobia (fear of homosexuals). AIDS was called the 'gay plague' and there were many people who saw the disease as God's judgement on sexual behaviour which, according to the Bible, is totally condemned.

This had catastrophic effects for those people suffering from AIDS. They were fast becoming the 20th century equivalent of the lepers mentioned in the Bible. Just as the wretched lepers were shunned by society, attempts were made to isolate AIDS sufferers. People reacted totally irrationally:

❖ parents kept their children away from one school which contained a child known to have the virus;
❖ insurance companies began to ask all kinds of personal questions about the sexual behaviour of men and women applying for a policy. If they admitted to being homosexual they were charged higher premiums;
❖ members of the congregation in more than one church refused to share the chalice in Holy Communion with those known to be HIV positive.

Almost every day brought new stories of prejudice and ignorance.

Questions about AIDS

The AIDS epidemic has forced society to ask many awkward and difficult questions about itself. Among them are the following:

A *In recent years the focus in the AIDS debate has been on caring for AIDS sufferers and their families and friends. What kind of help do you think they need?*

a) What is its attitude towards the gay community? There is clear evidence that many gay people have changed their sexual behaviour but far less evidence that the heterosexual population is prepared to do the same. The gay community has also looked after its many AIDS victims in a loving, caring and selfless way. Will the heterosexual community do the same?

b) How should those known to be HIV positive be treated? Should unborn babies known to have the virus be aborted? Should adults with the virus be isolated? How much money is the Health Service in the U.K. prepared to spend specifically on treatment of the disease and further research into it? How high is AIDS placed on its list of priorities?

c) Should people who have AIDS be allowed to move freely between different countries? In 1994 the Russian government decided to AIDS test all visitors to the country. Is this a good idea? Should other governments follow suit? What about movement within a country for AIDS sufferers? Should that be restricted?

d) What kind of practical help should the State give to those suffering from AIDS and those who care for them? At the moment almost all specialised help is given on a voluntary basis.

e) Should the sex education of children be given a higher priority? If so, at what age should that education begin and what should it contain? Should condoms be both readily available and free in workplaces, schools, colleges, clubs, etc. Should we become much more open about sex? Can young people be educated into adopting sensible patterns of sexual behaviour?

These are just a few questions that you could begin by asking. You can probably add many more to the list.

B Do you think that the AIDS crisis has forced people to think more seriously about safe sex?

ANSWER IN YOUR BOOK ...

1 How have society, and many Christians, dealt with the AIDS crisis?

2 How has the homosexual community dealt with the AIDS crisis?

3 How has Russia tried to deal with the AIDS epidemic?

WHAT DO YOU THINK?

A series of questions for you to think about. Try to come up with some answers.

a) Imagine that you had been entrusted by the British Government with the task of getting over to young people today the truth about AIDS and the message of safe sex. How would you try to do it?

b) Do you think that there is a great deal of mis-information about sex and AIDS circulating among young people? If so, what are some of these 'myths'?

c) Do you think that some people have used the AIDS crisis to reinforce some of the prejudices that they hold about homosexuals? Is homophobia common among young people in your experience?

d) Do you think that the Christian Church has a place in the debate within our society about sexual behaviour and the way that we must learn to live with AIDS? If so, what do you think that place is?

IN THE GLOSSARY ...

HIV; Homosexual; Homophobia; AIDS; Bible; Holy Communion; Heterosexual; Abortion; Condom.

7.5 EUTHANASIA

Euthanasia, the right to seek 'a good, easy death', arouses very strong emotions because it goes right to the heart of what we believe about both life and death. There are two approaches to the issue:

a) Those who argue that everyone has the right to expect a dignified exit from the world when their time comes. People have begun to speak of making 'Living Wills' when they are healthy which stipulate that their life should not be unnecessarily and artificially prolonged. Such Wills would then be binding on anyone treating them in the future.
b) Those who see any concession to euthanasia ('mercy killing') as a very dangerous path to tread. They maintain that life should be preserved at all costs and that euthanasia amounts to little less than murder.

Which of these particular arguments do you agree with? Can you explain why?

Euthanasia

The Voluntary Euthanasia Society (now called 'EXIT') has argued that everyone should have the opportunity to die under their own terms. In particular, it argues the following:

1 Faced with a terminal illness, for which there is no cure, everyone should be able to turn to: "...the mercy of a painless death."
2 If a patient requests it then a doctor should be able to assist him or her to end their own life.
3 As a safeguard, the patient should have signed a request to make this possible at least 30 days before it is administered.

EXIT states that every man and woman should have the right to seek to escape from a painful and useless existence. If they take this way out they are sparing friends and relatives from the unnecessary anguish of seeing their loved one in great pain. They are also saving scarce medical resources which could then be used to help those who can be cured.

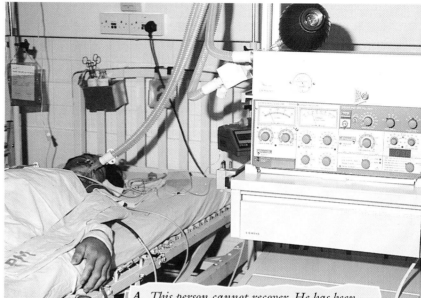

A *This person cannot recover. He has been classified as 'brain-dead'. Who do you think should take the decision to finally turn off the machine and end his life?*

B *We will look at the Hospice Movement in the next chapter. Before we do so, however, try to find out what is distinctive about the kind of care which nurses and doctors in a hospice offer to patients.*

The Roman Catholic Church, among others, have conducted a very aggressive campaign against making euthanasia legal. The main arguments put forward are the following:

a) There are now ways in which pain can be controlled and people can die with dignity. This has coincided with the growth of the Hospice Movement (see Unit 7.6). The control of pain by using drugs, which the Hospice Movement specialises in, is called 'palliative medicine'.

b) Only God has the right to decide when a person will die. In any case, people are not like animals. They cannot simply be 'put to sleep'. They have 'eternal souls' and the time of their coming and going is determined by God.

c) Doctors take the 'Hippocratic Oath' which binds them to saving life at all costs. Administering euthanasia is plainly against this.

d) People sometimes recover against all the odds.

In the Netherlands euthanasia is technically illegal but doctors can administer it without fear of prosecution. It is claimed that around 4000 deaths a year are caused by euthanasia. There are safeguards against abuse. The doctor involved must be able to show that:

- ❖ he or she carried out the wishes of the patient;
- ❖ he or she outlined fully the alternative courses of action available to the patient;
- ❖ a colleague was brought in for a second opinion.

Death is usually caused by fatal injection or tablets. The doctor's file is passed on to the police or coroner after death. The case may then be investigated if there are any suspicious circumstances.

ANSWER IN YOUR BOOK ...

1 What is euthanasia?

2 What is EXIT and what are its main arguments in favour of euthanasia?

3 What are the main arguments against euthanasia?

READ AND DECIDE ...

Here are two quotations for you to read and think about:

a) The Methodist Conference of 1974 stated that the argument for euthanasia would be met if:
"Medical skill in terminal care (is) improved, pre-death loneliness is relieved, patient and family are supported by the statutory services and the community. The whole of the patient's needs, including the spiritual, must be met."
- ❖ What do you understand by the phrase 'pre-death loneliness'?
- ❖ How do you think the patient and family should be supported at this time?
- ❖ What 'spiritual' needs does a person have as he or she approach the end of their life?

b) Dr Cicely Saunders, founder of the modern Hospice Movement, said the following:
"Anything which says to the very ill that they are a burden to their family and that they would be better off dead is unacceptable. What sort of society could let its old folk die because they are 'in the way'?"
- ❖ Is euthanasia a way of letting elderly people die because they are 'in the way'?
- ❖ Is euthansia for the benefit of others, as this quote suggests, or is it for the benefit of the dying person? Could the answer contain an element of both?

IN THE GLOSSARY ...

Euthanasia; Roman Catholic Church; Terminal Illness.

7.6 THE HOSPICE MOVEMENT

The first modern hospice was set up by Irish nuns, the Sisters of Charity, in Dublin towards the end of the 19th century. Then, in 1900, five of the nuns travelled to England and continued their work of caring for the dying in the East End of London. Within a few years they had established the St Joseph's Hospice. Almost sixty years after this a young nurse, Cicely Saunders, went to work at St Joseph's. Her nursing career was cut short by a serious back injury but she went on to establish many other hospices, starting with St Christopher's which was opened in 1969.

Now there are almost 100 in-patient hospices in England. At any one time they provide care for some 2000 patients, young and old, men and women. Most of the units are run by charities and many of them have a Christian basis although the patients in them are not necessarily all Christians.

The aims of the hospice movement

Whatever their background hospices have the same basic objective – to offer care and support for their patients and their patients relatives and friends at the most difficult stage in their lives. Within this overall objective there are three main aims:

a) *To relieve pain* – whether it is caused by the illness itself or by the stress and fear that it creates. Hospices specialise in pain control. Doctors and nurses in hospices have led the way in palliative medicine (pain control by drugs) in recent years. Hospices maintain that all pain, no matter how severe, can be brought under control.

b) *To enable patients and their families to face up to death* – to talk about their fears and anxieties in a free and open way. Providing the opportunities to talk about death is one of the main facilities offered by a hospice.

c) *To care for the emotional needs of relatives* – before, during and after the patient's death. In modern hospitals, the needs of those who survive are almost totally ignored. A hospice seeks to fulfil those needs.

A *There are six hospices in England devoted to the care of children and young people. What particular problems do you think they might encounter as they try to prepare them for death?*

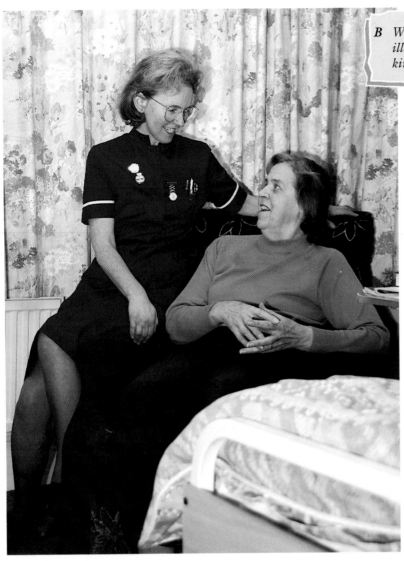

B *Why do you think that so many terminally ill patients derive great comfort from the kind of help offered by hospices?*

ANSWER IN YOUR BOOK ...

1 How did the modern hospice movement begin?
2 What is distinctive about the kind of care that hospices offer patients?
3 What does a hospice set out to do?

WHAT DO YOU THINK?

Six hospices in the U.K. are devoted to the care of terminally ill children and young people. One of these is Helen House, in Oxford. Its Director, Mother Frances Dominica, has explained how she sees the role of a children's hospice:

a) "A children's hospice is not, in the vast majority of cases, a place where children are taken to die. The definition of the word hospice is a place of shelter for pilgrims and travellers."
   ❖ What important point is Mother Frances making here?

b) "A children's hospice is to be alongside the family offering friendship, support and practical help; it can be seen as an artificial extended family..."
   ❖ What point is being made in the comparison between a hospice and an extended family?

c) "...by giving them permission to be who they are and ensuring that they are in a loving, supportive environment, it is possible to help them to meet death with a dignity and a nobility which in no way denies grief."
   ❖ How do you understand this rather surprising phrase: 'by giving them permission to be who they are...'?
   ❖ Mother Frances speaks of treating dying people 'with dignity'. What do you think she means by this?

IN THE GLOSSARY ...

Hospice Movement.

How hospices help

Most hospices can only offer fairly short-term care as the demand for their beds is considerable. To begin with, patients often just come for a week or two to give their carers a much-needed rest or holiday. Then, as their physical condition begins to decline, they have the alternative of spending a longer spell in the hospice. At the end of this time, they have the choice of whether to die at home or in the hospice. This is an important part of the hospice philosophy. It leaves the patient with a measure of independence and enables them to use the hospice facilities to come to terms with their impending death. Macmillan Nurses are attached to many hospices and these specialise in the care of cancer patients in their own homes. The emphasis is very much upon death with dignity, wherever that death takes place.

7.7 SUICIDE

A *When attempted suicide is described as a 'cry for help', what do you think is meant?*

Until 1961 suicide was illegal in the U.K. Someone who tried to take their own life, and failed, could find themselves being prosecuted. Now, attempted suicide is no longer an offence in the U.K. but it is still illegal to assist someone else to take their own life. Here are some facts and figures about suicide in the world today:

1 Some 1200 people in the world take their lives each day. This works out at a person every 1½ minutes.

2 Men are much more likely to attempt suicide than women.

3 The most vulnerable age-group for suicide is between the ages of 20 and 45. In recent years, however, the number of suicides by teenagers has increased dramatically.

4 About 1 in 10 people who fail in their attempt to commit suicide later succeed in doing so.

Reasons

Suicide is a very extreme measure to take. It usually takes desperate circumstances to bring a person to this point. The instinct for survival in all of us is, after all, extremely powerful. What, then, causes people to take their own lives?

a) *Personal worries:* loneliness, financial difficulties, fear of redundancy, anxiety about growing old, pressures at work or school, etc.

b) *Family worries:* bereavement, the threat of divorce, divorce itself, etc.

c) *Alcohol or drug abuse.*

d) *Mental instability.*

Those organisations working among men and women who are likely to attempt suicide, such as the Samaritans, tell us that suicide is often a 'cry for help'. If such help happens to be available at the time, there is a fair chance that the person can be persuaded not to attempt suicide.

The Samaritans

In 1953 the Reverend Chad Varah, a Church of England priest working in the East End of London, was horrified to discover how many people in his area were attempting to take their own lives. He installed a special telephone line in his vestry and soon found himself inundated with telephone calls asking for help. This was the beginning of a very important ministry. The Samaritans was born. Today there are over 180 branches of the Samaritans in the U.K. with telephones staffed by more than 21,000 trained volunteers. The organisation now deals with more than 300,000 telephone calls a year.

B Why do you think that so many people who are thinking of taking their own lives phone the Samaritans?

The Christian attitude

Christians believe that life is a sacred gift from God. Just as God bestowed this gift at conception so God, alone, can take this gift away at death. A person who tries to take his or her own life is, in a real sense, 'playing God'. The same argument is used, as we have seen, against euthanasia.

In the past the Church, especially the Roman Catholic Church, has taken a very strict line against suicide. It taught that a person who took their own life had committed a very 'grave' sin and could not go to heaven. Suicide victims were not buried in consecrated (holy) ground nor given a Church funeral. Nowadays, though, attitudes have changed. Most Christian churches seek to understand the pressures that have led to a person taking their own life and the support which is needed by friends and relatives who survive.

ANSWER IN YOUR BOOK ...

1 What are the main reasons behind people taking their own lives?
2 What is the 'Samaritans'?
3 What is the Christian attitude towards suffering?

READ AND DECIDE ...

Look up the parable of the Good Samaritan in Luke 10.30-37. Why do you think that Chad Varah chose this particular name for his telephone help-line?

WHAT DO YOU THINK?

All of the people who listen in on the telephones for the Samaritans are volunteers. After being accepted they go through a rigorous period of training. Before working for the organisation they need to accept certain uncomfortable 'truths', as this comment by a volunteer shows:

"Volunteers have to resist their natural impulse to solve some desperate cases by giving material comfort ... they have to accept that a client's sworn promise to phone next day is often not kept ... they have to accept that gratitude doesn't necessarily follow weeks and months of time spent on cases ... that often the person helped doesn't even remember his name. The volunteer discovers that he is what he actually chooses to be – faceless, nameless, just a voice or an ear and nothing more..."

With this information in mind, what kind of person do you think would be suited to be a Samaritan volunteer?

IN THE GLOSSARY ...

Euthanasia; Roman Catholic Church; Priest.

7.8 THE BIO-TECHNOLOGICAL REVOLUTION

We hear a great deal about the number of abortions, the problem of teenage pregnancy and the number of unwanted babies in the U.K. We hear far less, however, about another major problem – that of infertility. Yet 1 in 10 of all married couples in the U.K. cannot have a child because the mother or the father are infertile. This simply means the following:

a) The mother is unable to provide an egg each month for fertilisation. The most likely explanation for this is that her fallopian tubes are blocked or damaged, preventing the egg from making its way down into the uterus.

b) The father is not providing enough healthy sperm to fertilise his partner's egg. His 'sperm count' may be too low or many of the sperm may be substandard.

Whatever the reason for the couple's infertility, medical help is needed if they are going to be able to have a baby. Each year in the U.K. 20,000 couples undergo fertility treatment. There are three options open to them and each one of them raises important moral and ethical considerations.

AIH (Artificial insemination of the woman by her husband)

This happens when tests show that the father is healthy but the mother is not providing an egg for fertilisation. Sperms can then be taken from the husband and implanted in the wife's body. Fertilisation takes place and the pregnancy develops normally. Those opposed to any form of artificial insemination will argue that this is unnatural and against the will of God. Most people, however, look upon AIH as science simply giving a helping hand to a man and woman who cannot have a baby naturally.

A Do you think that the moment when a baby is conceived has anything to do with the activity and intervention of God or not?

AID (Artificial insemination of a woman using an unknown donor's sperm)

This can take place if a woman is fertile but her partner is infertile. One of the woman's eggs is fertilised by sperm taken from an anonymous donor. The fertilised egg is then put back into the woman's body and the pregnancy continues normally.

This raises more controversial questions in the minds of most people:

1 Can the husband and wife be considered to be the real parents of the child if the man was not involved in its conception?
2 Is AID really a sophisticated form of adultery, as many Christians claim?

IVF (In Vitro Fertilisation)

In this case the ovum (egg) is removed from a woman's body and fertilised by a man's sperm in a laboratory. The fertilised egg is them replaced in the woman's body. It was back in 1978 that the world's first 'test-tube' baby, Louise Brown, was conceived in this way and it is now a fairly common procedure. Two questions come to mind:

a) As long as the wife's egg and the husband's sperm are used, does it matter that conception takes place outside the woman's body?

b) Is there any difference if the egg is fertilised by a donor's sperm?

There are also other variations on this theme. There is 'surrogacy' (womb-leasing), where a woman gives birth to a baby for a wife who cannot conceive herself. There is also 'embryo donation', where a fertilised egg (with both donors unknown) is placed back into the wife's uterus because both she and her husband are infertile.

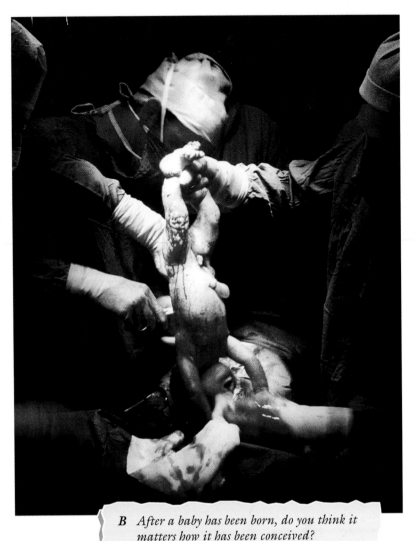

B *After a baby has been born, do you think it matters how it has been conceived?*

ANSWER IN YOUR BOOK ...

1 What is 'Artificial Insemination by Husband'?

2 What is 'Artificial Insemination by Donor'?

3 What is 'In Vitro Fertilisation'?

DISCUSS AMONG YOURSELVES...

This whole area of medical intervention in the reproductive field raises important questions. Here are some for you to discuss among yourselves:

a) If a couple are infertile, can that be seen as the will of God?

b) Should medical science interfere with the way that things are?

c) Is there any real objection to 'Artificial Insemination by Husband'?

d) If someone else's egg or sperm are involved in the pregnancy, do they have any rights over the baby that is conceived?

e) If someone else's egg or sperm are implanted in a woman's body, does it amount to the same thing as adultery?

FIND OUT AND NOTE ...

Interference with human fertility is an issue over which Christians strongly disagree. Try to find out what Roman Catholics and Anglicans believe about the following:
❖ AIH
❖ AID
❖ IVF

IN THE GLOSSARY ...

Abortion; Infertility; Fallopian Tubes; AIH; AID; IVF; Adultery; Surrogacy; Embryo; Uterus.

7.9 SUFFERING

In this book we have looked at many kinds of disability and suffering. We turn quite naturally now to consider the question of suffering as a whole. No other problem causes such acute distress to men and women who believe in a loving and caring God. Christians believe that God made, and sustains, all forms of life. Why, then, is there suffering? Much of it is undeserved and rarely serves any useful purpose.

Suffering

Suffering occurs in the modern world on a widespread and massive scale. We are now able to see such suffering almost as it happens. Take just three examples:

1 *Natural disasters (volcanoes, earthquakes, floods, etc)*. These are disasters over which human beings have little, if no, control. Yet such events have the capacity to kill millions of people. If human beings do not have any real power over nature who does?

2 *Hunger and malnutrition*. Hunger is directly responsible for the deaths of 20,000,000 children and adults in the world each year. Almost all of them die because they had the misfortune to be born in a part of the world which suffers continually from starvation.

3 *Incurable diseases or massive handicaps*. Through no fault of their own, or of their parents, thousands of babies are born each year with handicaps that will remain with them for the rest of their lives. Other people are struck down in the prime of life by an incurable illness. As a result, families are left fatherless or motherless.

There are many other examples of suffering and, no doubt, you could add some of your own thoughts to this list. It is not just the 'facts' of suffering that cause such anguish to Christian believers. It is also the 'unfairness' of it all. Some people suffer much more than others and there are many who have never known a moment free of pain and suffering. Why does it happen? Why is it all so unfair? Is there a purpose to it all? As far as God is concerned, the dilemma can be put quite simply:

A *When you see devastation like this on the television or in the newspapers, what questions does it raise in your mind?*

110

Either God wants to remove suffering but cannot – in which case he is not all-powerful.

Or God can remove suffering but will not – in which case he is not all-loving.

Christianity and Suffering

Suffering is an enormously complex problem. Here are four suggested solutions for you to think and talk about:

a) God alone knows the reason for suffering. Human beings simply have to accept what happens to them. One day they will know the reason why.

b) Suffering is a direct consequence of human sin in the world today.

c) Suffering arises from the activity of Satan, the Devil, in the world today.

d) Suffering occurs when human beings use their free-will in the wrong way.

To what extent do these answers meet, or fail to meet, the problems that suffering cause?

B *When you see a child or a young person with a handicap, what questions does it prompt you to ask?*

DISCUSS AMONG YOURSELVES...

There is no conclusive answer to the problem of suffering. You might decide, however, that some of the suggested answers in the text do provide us with some clues. Break up into small groups and look at each of these 'answers' together. Concentrate on the following questions:

a) What are the arguments that could be put forward to support each of the answers?

b) What are the arguments against each of the answers?

c) Do you find any of these answers more persuasive than the others. If so, why?

d) How would you explain the problem of suffering to somebody?

WRITE AN ESSAY ...

Write an essay of between 400 and 500 words with the following title:
   'Suffering – the Christian problem.'

ANSWER IN YOUR BOOK ...

1 Explain the dilemma that suffering causes the person who has a strong belief in God.

2 Which aspects of suffering do you think cause the most concern to the Christian believer?

3 What are some of the suggested answers to the problem of suffering that a Christian might put forward?

IN THE GLOSSARY ...

Natural Disaster.

8.1 THE UNIVERSAL DECLARATION OF HUMAN RIGHTS

One of the first acts of the newly formed United Nations was to draw up its Declaration of Human Rights. This it did on December 10th, 1948. In this Declaration the United Nations placed on record its belief that there are certain human rights which every man, woman and child must have, no matter where they are living. They cover civil, political, social and religious rights.

The Universal Declaration of Human Rights

The Declaration of Human Rights laid down the following objectives:

A *Which human rights do you appreciate most?*

- ❖ All human beings are born free and equal in dignity and rights.

- ❖ Everyone is entitled to these human rights without any distinction of race, colour, sex or religion.

- ❖ Everyone has the right to life, liberty and security of person.

- ❖ No one shall be held in slavery.

- ❖ No one shall be subject to torture, arbitrary arrest, detention or exile.

- ❖ All are equal before the law and have the right to a free, fair and public trial.

- ❖ Everyone charged with a criminal offence has the right to be presumed innocent until proved guilty.

- ❖ Everyone has the right to move around freely, both in their own country and abroad.

- ❖ Men and women of a full age have the right to marry and have a family, regardless of their race or religion. Both men and women are entitled to equal rights within marriage.

- ❖ Everyone has the right to own property of their own. The State does not have the right to take that property away arbitrarily.

- ❖ Everyone has the right to freedom of thought, opinion, conscience and religion. They also have the right to be able to express these opinions publicly.

- ❖ Everyone has the right to come together with other like-minded people in a peaceful assembly and to join associations or unions if they so wish.

- ❖ Everyone has the right to play a part in the governing of their country, whether at a local or a national level.

- ❖ Everyone has the right to work in paid employment and to be given a reasonable wage for the work they are doing.

- ❖ Everyone has the right to reasonable rest and leisure and to holidays with pay.

- ❖ Everyone has the right to enjoy an adequate level of education and to see such education provided for their children.

- ❖ Everyone has the right to expect that their basic needs will be met. These include housing, medical care and social security when they are ill or old.

- ❖ Everyone has the right to play a part in any cultural activities which take place in the community and to share in the economic and scientific advances which that community makes.

These 'rights' belong to everyone, irrespective of their colour, race, sex, religion, social class or place of birth. They should be able to enjoy them simply because they are a member of the human race. In return for these basic rights every human being must fully respect and recognise the rights, freedom, and needs of others.

Every member of the United Nations signed up to indicate their support for the Declaration. Sadly, many of those nations have been the very ones that have denied human rights to their citizens since.

C A refugee village. Can you find out what a refugee is? Why are refugees denied some of the most basic of all human rights?

B In almost every country of the world the proportion of elderly citizens in the population is increasing. What human rights do you think elderly people have?

ANSWER IN YOUR BOOK ...

1 Why do you think that one of the first acts of the newly formed United Nations was to draw up a Declaration on Human Rights?

2 What do you think are the most basic of all human rights?

3 Why do you think that many governments deny such human rights to their citizens?

FIND OUT AND NOTE ...

Prince Sadruddin Aga Khan was the United Nations Commissioner for Refugees. Concerning human rights he said the following:

"The rights to life, to an adequate standard of living, to freedom of expression, to protection from torture, inhuman treatment, or arbitrary arrest, and many of the common standards of achievement for all peoples and nations are as far from realisation as ever."

a) Do you agree with the Prince's statement that human rights are still being denied to people all over the world? If so, can you explain why a basic level of dignity for all human beings seems impossible to reach?

b) In the next few weeks collect as many examples as you can from the mass media which illustrate the basic denial of human rights. Then write an essay of between 500 and 600 words on:
'The denial of human rights in the modern world.'

8.2 HUMAN RIGHTS

Many countries pay lip service to 'Human Rights' but show little commitment in practice. Even countries which belong to the United Nations are sometimes guilty of actions which go against the Declaration of Human Rights. They may discriminate against minority groups in their communities; prevent their people from speaking or meeting openly; imprison people without trial or use torture as a normal part of their legal system. The Declaration of Human Rights is based upon the principle that everyone in the world is equal and so entitled to be treated in the same way. For Christians this is also a Biblical principle. Here are four examples:

1 The teaching of Jesus that his followers should ''love your neighbour as you love yourself' (Matthew 22.39). The 'neighbour' of which Jesus spoke was everybody, without exception.
2 The teaching of Jesus that when one of his followers helps the sick and needy or visits someone in prison, they are doing that action to Jesus himself (Matthew 25.31-46).
3 The parable of the Good Samaritan (Luke 10.25-37) which teaches that helping other people in need should be carried out irrespective of their nationality or religion.
4 The reminder by James that faith without action is dead (James 2.17). True faith in God must lead to genuine action for those in need.

Amnesty International

By its very nature the denial of human rights to an individual, or a group of people, is likely to be carried out in secret. Amnesty International was formed in 1961 by the British lawyer, Peter Benenson, to bring any violations of human rights out into the open. Since then the organisation, which now has over 1,000,000 members worldwide, seeks to highlight the different ways in which basic human rights are being denied throughout the world. In particular, it seeks to secure the following:

a) The abolition of the death penalty in all countries. Over eighty countries have retained the death penalty for acts of terrorism and certain categories of murder but it has recently been introduced by countries like Singapore and Malaysia for such crimes as drug-trafficking.

A *Do you find it quite astonishing that people are still doing this to other human beings in the 20th century? Do you think that there is anything at all that can be done to stop it happening?*

b) The abolition of torture as a means of gaining information from people in captivity. Countries ruled by dictators, in particular, are likely to employ torture frequently.

c) A fair and speedy trial for all people arrested while making sure that they are legally represented. This is particularly important for those people held for committing 'political' crimes.

d) The release of all 'prisoners of conscience' throughout the world. A 'prisoner of conscience' is someone in prison, or under 'house arrest', for what they believe, not what they have done.

Violations of Human Rights

In many countries, such as Iraq and China, there are frequent abuses of human rights. The opening days of 1995, for instance, brought news that thieves and Army deserters in Iraq were being punished by having their hands and feet chopped off. In other countries, Amnesty International has also criticised aspects of the legal system or law. Britain, for example, has been criticised in recent years for the way that remand prisoners (i.e: prisoners in prison awaiting trial) have been treated and for the fact that immigrants have been prevented from joining their direct relatives in Britain.

The Action by Christians against Torture (ACT) is a much smaller organisation than Amnesty International but it seeks to express a specifically Christian concern about the use of torture in the modern world. It argues that its use is contrary to everything that Christians believe about God and the human race.

ANSWER IN YOUR BOOK ...

1 Why should Christians be very concerned when they hear about people being abused in today's world?

2 Why was Amnesty International formed?

3 Which violations of human rights has Amnesty International objected to in particular?

FIND OUT AND NOTE ...

Find out as much as possible about the worldwide work of Amnesty International.

B Why do you think that the logo of this organisation shows a flame surrounded by barbed wire?

READ AND DECIDE ...

A leaflet published by Amnesty International defines the aims of the organisation:

"Amnesty International is engaged in what is often a life or death struggle to defend human rights in many countries all over the world ... Only by becoming a mass movement for human rights can we hope to play our full part in ending the international hypocrisy which surrounds the plight of so many – those who suffer alone or collectively amidst a deafening silence from some of the very people who pay lip service to the Universal Declaration of Human Rights. ... Amnesty's sole reason for existence (is) to campaign against torture and execution and for the release of men and women imprisoned for their beliefs, colour, ethnic origin, language or religion ... it is the inalienable right of people to exercise freedom of speech, association or organisation without fear..."

a) Amnesty International is an international organisation looking at violations of human rights on a worldwide scale. Why is its very existence necessary in today's world?

b) Why do you think that many countries only pay 'lip service' to the United Nations Declaration of Human Rights?

c) What would you describe as the 'sole reason' for Amnesty International's existence?

IN THE GLOSSARY ...

Bible; Prisoner Of Conscience.

8.3 WOMEN'S RIGHTS

There is an enormous difference between the treatment of men and women worldwide. Here are some basic facts:

Women:
- ❖ make up 52% of the world's population;
- ❖ do 65% of the world's work;
- ❖ produce 50% of the world's food;
- ❖ receive 10% of the world's income;
- ❖ own 1% of the world's property.

Men:
- ❖ make up 48% of the world's population;
- ❖ own 99% of the world's property;
- ❖ make up over 90% of national and local government representatives;
- ❖ earn an average of 25% more than women for doing identical jobs.

In the Developing World women are expected to combine domestic work, child-rearing and exhausting physical work. In the Developed World women are gradually breaking down traditional attitudes. However, this is only happening very slowly. While some women play active roles in business and industry well over 90% of the top positions in the U.K. are still occupied by men.

The Sex Discrimination Act, 1975

Since 1975 it has been unlawful in the U.K. to discriminate against either men or women in the areas of:
- ❖ Recruitment to work
- ❖ Promotion in work
- ❖ Training for work

In the same year the Employment Protection Act made

A *Why do you think that so few companies are willing to provide creche facilities for the children of their employees?*

it illegal to dismiss a woman because she had become pregnant. Under the Act, every pregnant worker was entitled to maternity leave if she wanted to take it. Why, then, are there far fewer women in top jobs in the U.K. than men? There are several possible reasons:

a) Many women find it very difficult to combine a demanding job with bringing up children, particularly when a child is ill. If a business thinks that pregnancy is a distinct possibility in the future, it might be unwilling to appoint a woman to a top position.

b) The current employment situation takes little account of the needs of women employees. Few companies, for instance, offer creche facilities for mothers with young children. There has only been a limited willingness among companies to offer female employees flexible working hours to fit in with the school-hours of children.

c) Maternity leave is expensive for a company which needs to find a trained replacement. The mother who returns may also find herself out-of-touch and need re-training. For many companies it is easier, and cheaper, to appoint a man in the first place.

B *Things will not change in the lifetime of this old woman. What about her children and grandchildren?*

The problem of prejudice against women goes back a long way. In the Old Testament men were given the dominant role in Jewish society and we find this carried over into the teaching of the early Christian Church. St Paul, for example, insisted that women should keep silent within the Christian community and accept the dominance of their husbands within the marriage relationship (1.Timothy 2.8-15).

Later, Church leaders carried this much further, finding little that was positive to say about the female sex. One of them, Clement of Alexandria, declared:

> "Every woman should be overwhelmed with shame at the thought that she is a woman."

The dominance of the man, and the subservience of the woman, has continued in the Christian Church to the present time. The stranglehold was only partially broken in the Church of England by the decision to ordain women (see Unit 8.4).

WHAT DO YOU THINK?

Many people believe that a woman should be a mother first and a worker second.

a) Do you agree with this attitude?

b) If someone tries to fulfil both roles at the same time will there inevitably be a conflict?

c) Do you think there are ways in which a woman can reconcile her roles of mother and worker? If so, how?

d) Do you think that society could do more to help women who want to have a family yet continue working? If so, how?

ANSWER IN YOUR BOOK ...

1 How unbalanced is the situation between men and women in today's world?

2 What did the Sex Discrimination Act and the Employment Protection Act set out to achieve?

3 Why do many women find it difficult, or impossible, to hold down a demanding job?

IN THE GLOSSARY ...

Old Testament; Paul.

8.4 THE ORDINATION OF WOMEN

When the Sex Discrimination Act was passed in 1975 some exceptions were allowed. Among the exceptions was the acceptance that the Church might have its own reasons for not ordaining women to the priesthood.

The Ordination of women

For almost 2000 years the Christian Church has solidly maintained a male priesthood. Many people have seen this as a blatant example of men wishing to retain spiritual power in their own hands. At times, the Church has been at the forefront of those wishing to keep women suppressed in our society.

During the 20th century, however, cracks in this male domination have appeared and different Churches have gradually admitted women to the priesthood. Today, nearly all of the Protestant Churches (the Church of England and the Free Churches) admit women to the priesthood and some elect them to positions of leadership. The Salvation Army, for instance, has been led on more than one occasion by a woman Commissioner. Anglicans in Canada, the U.S.A. and New Zealand have ordained women for some years. They are not, however, allowed to officiate as priests in those countries which do not have women priests. In 1989 Anglicans in the U.S.A. chose their first woman bishop and the Pope wrote to the Archbishop of Canterbury pointing out that this would be a great obstacle towards Church unity. We will find out why in a moment.

The major decision was that taken by the Church of England in 1992. The issue had been regularly discussed in the Church for many years but the decision to admit women priests was finally taken, by a very small majority, after a long and bitter debate. The first women were ordained in 1994.

The Roman Catholic Church and the ordination of women

In 1976 the Roman Catholic Church outlined its opposition to the ordination of women:

a) Christianity has always held to the tradition, first established by Christ and his apostles, that only men should belong to the priesthood. Jesus chose only men to be his apostles – and bishops, deacons and priests gain their authority from the apostles.

b) At Mass, the central act of Catholic worship, the priest represents Christ himself. The Roman Catholic Church argues that only a man can do this. Men are not better than women but there is a difference in the roles that God calls them to play.

c) Many within the Church may want to see women ordained but the Church reflects the will of God. The Holy Scriptures and the Tradition of the Church are both clear in their teaching that women cannot be ordained. To deny this would be to undermine the whole authority of the Church.

A *Find out all that you can about the process which led to the ordination of women into the Church of England in 1994.*

The Roman Catholic Church will not ordain women to the priesthood, no matter what the other Christian Churches have done in the past or will do in the future. Pope John Paul II has recently made it clear that this will continue to be the teaching of the Catholic Church. The fact that other Churches choose to do so is a major obstacle towards the eventual reunion of the Christian Church worldwide.

B Invite a woman priest into your class to talk about the whole issue of women's ordination. Try to find out why the move was so strongly opposed.

ANSWER IN YOUR BOOK ...

1 Which Churches now admit women to the priesthood?

2 When did the Anglican Church take the decision to admit women to the priesthood? When were the first women ordained?

3 What are the main reasons behind the Roman Catholic Church's continued refusal to ordain women?

IN YOUR OWN WORDS ...

Define each of the following words, used in this chapter, as briefly as possible:

a) Protestant

b) Priest

c) Anglican

d) Pope

e) Archbishop of Canterbury

WHAT DO YOU THINK?

1 Why do you think that the Sex Discrimination Act of 1975 should make an exception for the Christian Church over the issue of women's ordination?

2 Why do you think that Jesus did not include any women among his apostles? Do you think that this omission is significant?

3 Why do you think that the Pope saw the admittance of women to the priesthood of the Church of England as a great obstacle in the path of future unity between the Churches?

IN THE GLOSSARY ...

Protestant; Salvation Army; Priest; Anglican Church; Pope; Archbishop Of Canterbury.

8.5 THE RIGHTS OF CHILDREN

A *What rights do you think this child, and all children, have?*

Until the 20th century the idea of children having 'rights' at all would have seemed ridiculous to most people. Children were viewed as being the 'property' of their parents, unable to think or speak for themselves. They were forced to work long hours in factories or mines. It was not until 1922 that Eglantyne Webb, the founder of the Save the Children Fund, drafted a Charter to cover the 'Rights of the Child'. For the first time the 'Rights' of every child in the world, regardless of their nationality, race or religion were spelled out. Included among those 'Rights' were that:

a) no child shall be exploited by others;
b) every child shall be given the opportunity to mature physically, mentally and emotionally in their own time;
c) each child should be taught to offer a life of service to others.

In 1959 the United Nations adopted its own 'Declaration of the Rights of the Child'. It began by saying that "...mankind owes to the child the best it has to give..." before going on to say that every child has the right to expect the following:

a) Special protection and opportunities to help them grow physically, spiritually, socially and emotionally.
b) A name and a nationality.
c) Adequate nutrition, housing, recreation and medical services.
d) Special medical treatment if needed.
e) Love, care and protection from parents or some other appointed body.
f) Protection in times of disaster and from all forms of cruelty and neglect.
g) Protection from any form of discrimination based on race or religion.

In drafting this Declaration the members of the United Nations had three kinds of danger to children and young people in mind:

1 *Danger from war.* Modern warfare does not distinguish between soldiers and civilians. In recent wars millions of women and children have been killed. In many, such as the civil war in Rwanda (1993),

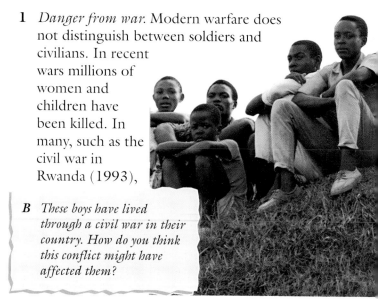

B *These boys have lived through a civil war in their country. How do you think this conflict might have affected them?*

120

were orphaned after their parents were killed. War not only deprives children of a normal childhood but also leaves them physically, mentally and emotionally scarred for life. In some countries, children as young as seven years old are drafted into the armed forces to be trained as soldiers.

2 *Danger from the State.* In many countries in recent years children have been arrested, tortured and even killed. Many have been abused because of their parents' political or religious beliefs. Back in 1977 Amnesty International reported that at least 300 children had been held as hostages and tortured.

3 *Danger from sexual and other forms of abuse.* Adults abuse children in all countries of the world. In the U.K., such abuse has received much attention lately although it is almost impossible to estimate its extent. Probably some 20% of children are physically, sexually or emotionally abused by their parents, or other adults, in some way. Elsewhere, children end up on the streets to beg or work as prostitutes. In countries such as India child labour is widely practised and is a modern form of slavery.

Who helps?

There are many national and international organisations which campaign to protect children. Among the most well-known are:

a) *The NSPCC (National Society for the Prevention of Cruelty to Children).* Founded in 1884 the NSPCC works to protect and look after children in Britain. Their duties include fundraising; mounting educational projects; setting up family care centres and instigating child protection schemes. The NSPCC's child protection officers may be called in to investigate reported cases of child abuse or neglect.

b) *Save the Children Fund.* This charity provides funds and personnel to look after the needs of children around the world. It also responds when children are the victims of an emergency or disaster.

ANSWER IN YOUR BOOK ...

1 Describe the three basic objectives of the Save the Children Fund when it was first set up in 1922.

2 Outline the United Nations Declaration of the Rights of the Child. If you could isolate three of these 'rights' as being most important, which would you choose? Why?

3 What are the main dangers for children in the world today?

FIND OUT AND NOTE ...

Carry out your own research into the work of **either** the NSPCC or Save the Children Fund. In particular, try to find out the following:

a) How and why the organisation came into existence in the first place.

b) The aims and principles on which the organisation is based.

c) The areas of need in which the organisation is particularly involved.

WHAT DO YOU THINK?

In this chapter you have encountered two separate Charters setting out the rights of children. Draw up your own Charter for children and young people adding a brief explanation why each item is, in your opinion, very important.

IN THE GLOSSARY ...

United Nations.

8.6 ANIMAL RIGHTS

Animals have been kept in captivity, and domesticated, for at least 4000 years. Recently, however, there has been a marked change in public attitudes towards animals and the way they are treated. This has been partly due to such developments as 'factory farming', which have caused people to ask some very searching questions. At the same time, traditional leisure pastimes such as fox-hunting and hare-coursing have come under the spotlight, leading to some strong and often violent protests.

Serious moral and spiritual questions have been asked about four aspects of the way that we treat animals in the modern world:

a) *Animals in captivity*. Humans have used animals for work purposes – husky dogs pulling sledges, dogs rounding up sheep, horses pulling ploughs – for centuries. Since Victorian times, people have also paid money to see animals in captivity (zoos) and performing (circuses). Most circuses today do not use animals and many zoos are finding that they have to concentrate a lot more on conservation work to justify their existence. The attitude of the general public towards both has changed considerably.

b) *Animals for food*. Some people (vegetarians) do not eat meat or animal products at all. Although this is not an attitude specifically encouraged in the Bible, many Christians are vegetarians. Most people do eat meat although they are beginning to ask more and more questions about the ways in which animals are reared and slaughtered. Can there be any possible justification for:
  ❖ … penning animals up (factory farming) and totally controlling their light, heat, ventilation, exercise and food intake?
  ❖ … keeping hens in cramped conditions with everything controlled to increase their egg production?
  ❖ … shipping young cattle abroad so that they can be reared in veal crates before being slaughtered?

c) *Animals for research*. Nearly 4,000,000 separate experiments are carried out on animals in scientific laboratories each year. 80% of these are performed without anaesthetic. Many of them are conducted in the course of medical research but the majority are still performed by cosmetic companies. 250,000 animals – including rats, monkeys, cats and dogs – die each year as a result of these experiments. The value of medical experiments on animals is often over-emphasised and it is difficult to find any justification for cosmetic experiments on animals. At the very least, stricter controls are required. Perhaps some forms of experiments should be banned completely. What do you think?

d) *Hunting animals*. People hunt and shoot animals for fun. Fox-hunting and stag-hunting have been part of the English way of life for centuries. Rearing and shooting birds, pheasants and wild fowl is big business. Millions are killed each year. The claim is often made that the hunting and killing of animals is a valuable service to the countryside but, as yet, the claim is unproven. What do you think the real reason is?

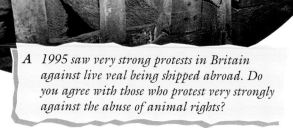

A 1995 saw very strong protests in Britain against live veal being shipped abroad. Do you agree with those who protest very strongly against the abuse of animal rights?

A Christian perspective

The Bible assumes that people will kill and eat animals. The two stories of creation in Genesis 1 and 2 assume that man will 'rule over' the fish, birds and every other living thing. Quite what the phrase 'rule over' was intended to mean no one is quite sure. Obviously, the human race was seen as God's 'steward' on earth, entrusted with the responsibility of putting God's intentions into practice. This is the God who, we are often told, is like a 'shepherd' to his people:

> "…he will carry the lambs in his bosom and lead the ewes to water."
> (Isaiah 40.11)

We are not told what God the Shepherd would have thought of factory farming, cosmetic experiments on animals and fox-hunting. What do you think?

B *Carry out some research to discover just what people feel about hunting animals.*

ANSWER IN YOUR BOOK …

1 What is vegetarianism?
2 What questions are raised by the carrying out of experiments on animals?
3 What is the Christian perspective on the way that animals should be treated?

USE YOUR IMAGINATION …

The use of animals in laboratory experiments is very controversial. However, suppose that a cure for the most common causes of cancer and a vaccine against the HIV virus were discovered as a result of experiments carried out on animals. Would you support such experiments? Do you think that experiments on animals for strict medical purposes are acceptable. Form your arguments clearly and explain your answer.

WHAT DO YOU THINK?

a) Animals are slaughtered for food to meet the requirements of the meat eating population. If the population objected strongly, and refused to buy, then practices would change. Do you think people care enough to do this?

b) Meat can be bought from animals which have been reared naturally and slaughtered humanely. It is, however, rather more expensive. Do you think that people care enough to pay the extra money?

c) Free range eggs can be bought but, once again, they are rather more expensive. Do you think that people care enough to just buy free range eggs?

d) Does it matter that most Christians continue to eat meat, no matter how it has been produced? Should Christians take more care?

IN THE GLOSSARY …

Bible; Vegetarian.

9.1 WHY DO PEOPLE FIGHT?

War, and the use of military aggression, is one of the greatest problems facing the human race in the modern world. More people have died in wars during the Twentieth Century than in the remainder of history. As we have developed 'better' and 'more efficient' weapons, we have increased our ability to kill people on a greater scale than ever before. Let us look at some statistics:

1 Since 1900 it is thought that some 100 million people, soldiers and civilians, have died as a result of war. 9,000,000 died in the First World War (1914-18) and 55,000,000 in the Second World War (1939-45).
2 At least five times as many people have been injured in military conflicts as have been killed. Over 21,000,000 men alone were injured in the First World War.
3 The balance of casualties has changed considerably as better weapons have been developed. In the First World War 95% of all casualties were soldiers. In the Second World War over 50% of the casualties were civilians while in most modern civil wars, over 90% of those killed and injured are civilians.

Why do people fight?

Apart from the deaths and injuries, modern warfare inflicts suffering on a far wider scale. In the 20th century warfare has deprived millions of their homes, making them refugees. Take just one example. When the Russian army moved into Afghanistan in 1979, thousands of people were made homeless. By the time that it left, in 1989, over 50% of the total population had become refugees. Hospitals, schools, offices and water supplies were also disrupted or destroyed.

Why, then, do people fight when the cost is so high? There are many reasons and to help us understand these we must divide war into different categories:

a) *Civil wars and 'wars of liberation'*. These can take one of two forms:
  ❖ Different political groups within a country may disagree to such an extent that they start fighting. Often, one of the parties sees itself as fighting a 'war of liberation' against the government. In recent years there have been 'civil wars' in such countries as Sudan, Afghanistan, El Salvador and Rwanda. The human cost of these wars has been immense with millions of people killed, injured or made homeless.
  ❖ Sometimes a country declares itself to be independent only to find itself under siege from a powerful, outside force. This happened in 1995 in Chechnya, formerly a part of Russia.

b) *Disputes over frontiers and borders.* Sometimes two countries lay claim to disputed land on the border between them. Occasionally, as in a long standing dispute between Greece and Turkey, the disagreement is over water rather than land.

A *Do you think the fact that most of the casualties of modern wars are civilians should alter the way that we look at war?*

Usually, valuable commodities such as oil or gas are at the heart of the dispute.

c) *Wars between nations.* These wars often arise because of frontier disputes, different political beliefs or because one country lays claim to another. Since 1945 there have been wars in the Middle East and South East Asia including the Korean War (1950-53); the Vietnam War (1965-73); the war between Iran and Iraq (1980-88) and the Gulf War (1991). Often, the world's superpowers (particularly the U.S.A., Britain and France) find themselves drawn in. Since 1945 only one year has passed, 1968, when the British Army has not been involved in an armed conflict.

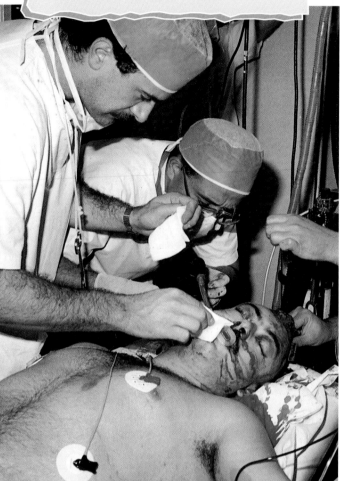

B *Just one of the many modern casualties of war. Try to find out what 'patriotism' is and explain why it plays a major part in war.*

C *This banner illustrates a verse from the prophet Isaiah (11.6). What do you think it has to do with war?*

ANSWER IN YOUR BOOK ...

1 Can you explain why far more civilians are killed in modern warfare than soldiers?

2 What is a civil war?

3 Why is the refugee problem almost always a large factor of modern warfare?

DISCUSS AMONG YOURSELVES...

Here are two quotations for you to think and talk about. They are taken from Jewish and Muslim holy books:

a) **Jewish Talmud:** "If a person intends to kill you, be first to kill him."

b) **Muslim Quran:** "Fight in the way of Allah (God) with those who fight you but do not begin hostilities."

According to these quotations, when is a person justified in going to war? Do you agree with this teaching?

WHAT DO YOU THINK?

Jesus suggested that there would never be a time when the world is free from war and violence:

"The time is coming when you will hear of wars and rumours of wars. See that you are not alarmed. Such things are bound to happen; but the end is still to come. For nation will go to war against nation, kingdom against kingdom..." (Matthew 24.6,7)

Can you ever see a time coming when war will be a thing of the past and different nations will learn to cooperate with one another? Before you form your answer, look at Isaiah 11.6 and decide whether this verse has anything to offer to the debate.

IN THE GLOSSARY ...

Refugee; Civil War.

9.2 JUST AND HOLY WARS

There are two approaches to war which have played a very important role in the history of the Christian Church.

The Just War

This attitude to war has a very long history. War can never be right but it might, on occasions, be less wrong than not going to war. Justice might demand a war and, as long as the war is fought by certain 'rules', it can be described as 'just'.

The roots of this idea are to be found in the old Roman Empire. The 'Christian' Emperor, Constantine, was convinced that God had given him victory in battle over his rival for the throne. Then, in 1250 CE, the Dominican friar and Church Father, St Thomas Aquinas (1225-74), laid down the four conditions which he felt justified a war. If they were met, any Christian could fight with a clear conscience:

1 There must be a just cause for war. In practice, this can only happen when a country is attacked and so needs to defend itself.
2 Every other possibility of solving the conflict must have been tried before a war is declared, including extensive negotiations.
3 The war must have a clear and just aim and all fighting must stop when that aim has been achieved.

4 The war must be fought in a just way. This means that:
   ❖ certain weapons will be outlawed;
   ❖ only as much force as is necessary to achieve victory must be used;
   ❖ no violence must be directed against civilians.

Do you think that it is possible to control war in this way? Certainly, these conditions would rule out almost all modern wars with the exception of the Second World War. Even then acts took place, such as the dropping of the atomic bombs on Japan and blanket bombing of German cities such as Dresden, which went way beyond these conditions.

The Holy War

In the 13th century BCE, the Israelites were led by Moses out of Egyptian slavery and taken towards the Promised Land of Canaan. After the Israelites had crossed the Red Sea and the waters had come together to swallow up the Egyptians, Moses led the people in a song of celebration. It contained these words:

> "I shall sing to the Lord, for he has risen in triumph;
> horse and rider he has hurled into the sea…
> The Lord is a warrior; the Lord is his name.
> Pharoah's chariots and his army
> he has cast into the sea…" (Exodus 15.1,2)

A *Do you see something dangerous in the notion of God leading an army into battle and giving them victory over their enemies?*

B *Why is this particular photograph an ironical comment on war?*

The implication is clear. God is the supreme 'warrior' who has given a mighty victory to his Chosen People. The Israelites believed that he continued to do so on many occasions as they set about conquering the Promised Land.

The Roman Emperor, Constantine, saw God in much the same light. Having won a victory against overwhelming odds he insisted that a standard carrying the symbol of a cross went before his army into every battle. Centuries later, a similar standard preceded the armies of the 'Christian' Crusaders as they fought the 'infidels', or 'pagans', who had occupied the Holy Land. Responding to a sermon delivered by the Pope they believed the following:

a) They were fighting for a holy and noble cause.
b) They were being directed in battle by God.
c) God was on their side because they were on His. It followed, then, that the soldiers who opposed them were the enemies of God.
d) Just as the Israelites destroyed everything, including the enemy, at the command of God, so they should do likewise.

We can see here all the elements of a 'Holy War'. Any army which believes that it is fighting for a noble cause will claim that its war is holy. Any soldier that believes this will willingly surrender his life. For soldiers fighting in the Crusades, the assurance by the Pope that they would have immediate eternal life was the only promise they needed.

ANSWER IN YOUR BOOK ...

1 What are the roots of the Christian idea of a 'Just War'?
2 Which conditions did St Thomas Aquinas lay down before a war could be called 'just'?
3 What is a 'Holy War'?

READ AND DECIDE ...

Read this comment about the 'Just War' carefully:
"War or violent struggle can never be just except in the very special circumstances that it is the only way of restraining a very great injustice; that it will not itself bring about greater destruction than the evil it opposes; that it has a reasonable chance of success; that it does not involve acts of injustice such as the deliberate killing of non-combatants and that those who wage it are authorised to do so by a large degree of popular support."
(Hebert. The Teaching of the Catholic Church)

a) What is a 'Just War'?
b) How do the conditions laid down in this extract compare with those given by St Thomas Aquinas?
c) Can you think of any problems which a country might encounter in trying to meet all five of these conditions for a 'Just War'? Do you think that they could be applied to a modern conflict? Could they be applied to a nuclear war? Give reasons for your answer.

IN THE GLOSSARY ...

Pacifism; Just War; Constantine; Pope; Holy War; Moses; Promised Land; Crusades.

9.3 NUCLEAR WAR

On August 6th, 1945 two Japanese cities, Hiroshima and Nagazaki, were destroyed by atomic bombs dropped by the U.S.A. An estimated 140,000 people died in the explosions while thousands more suffered from the dreadful after-effects of radiation. Thankfully, this is the only time that nuclear weapons have been used in war. It brought the Second World War to an end.

The bombs that were dropped on these two cities were tiny by modern standards, containing some 13,000 tonnes of dynamite. Modern nuclear warheads can carry an explosive force of more than 10,000,000 tonnes of dynamite. No-one knows the full extent of the world's nuclear arsenal but it is thought to be somewhere in the region of 10,000 million tonnes of dynamite.

The Arms Race

In 1945 only the U.S.A. was capable of producing nuclear weapons. It was not long, however, before other countries developed the raw materials and technology that were necessary to join the 'Nuclear Club'. The basic ingredient needed is plutonium, which is produced by nuclear reactors. Any country with such reactors to produce energy has the capacity to produce its own nuclear weapons.

Soon the 'Club' expanded. In 1949 the U.S.S.R. developed and tested its own nuclear weapons. An Arms Race developed between the U.S.S.R. and the U.S.A. as both sides competed against each other to produce yet more powerful and sophisticated weapons. Within a very short time the 'Nuclear Club' had five members – the U.S.A., the U.S.S.R., France, the U.K. and China. The 'Club' is now much larger and is thought to include Iran, Israel, South Africa, Egypt, Pakistan, India and North Korea among others. It is also thought that other countries will have the potential to produce nuclear weapons within the next few years.

Starting a nuclear war

Although there have been over 250 localised wars in the 50 years since the end of the Second World War, there has been no world war. Some people argue that this has been brought about by the presence of nuclear

A *Arthur Koestler, an American author, said that the arrival of nuclear weapons has changed the way that we see the world more than any other event in history. What do you think he meant? Do you agree with his comment?*

B *Protests like these were once commonplace. If nuclear weapons still exist, why do you think people have stopped protesting against them?*

weapons in the world. The devastation that would occur if such weapons were used would be almost incalculable. Others are not so sure. They point out that the world is still a very dangerous place with at least 20 nations having nuclear weapons – or the capacity to make them. A nuclear war (Third World War) could begin in the following circumstances:

a) A technical error set off a nuclear weapon accidentally.
b) An irresponsible government or terrorist group was able to get hold of a nuclear weapon.
c) A crazy dictator came to power in one of the countries which has the nuclear bomb.
d) A war fought with ordinary weapons suddenly escalated into a nuclear war.

There is reason to believe that the world has been very fortunate to escape the use of nuclear weapons on more than one occasion in the past. You might like to find out about the Cuban Missile crisis, for example, in the early 1960s which brought the world to the very brink of a nuclear conflict.

A final point needs to be made. Although many nuclear weapons have been destroyed since the collapse of the U.S.S.R. a vast number still remain and money continues to be spent on developing them. In 1992 alone, for example, the British government spent £23.5 billion on defence whilst giving away just 10% of this figure to help the poorer nations of the world.

ANSWER IN YOUR BOOK ...

1 Where were the first atomic bombs dropped and what effect did they have?
2 What is the 'Nuclear Club' and who belongs to it?
3 What is the 'Arms Race'?

READ AND DECIDE ...

Here are two comments for you to think about:

a) "Nuclear deterrence has kept the peace for 40 years and a non-nuclear world would be much more dangerous. The temptation for the superpowers to use some of the many nasty conventional chemical or biological weapons at their disposal would be increased..." **(Editorial in Sunday Times. 19.1.1986)**
❖ There appear to be at least two misconceptions in this brief extract. Can you identify them?

b) "Before the bomb, man had to live with the idea of his death as an individual; from now onwards, mankind has to live with the idea of death as a species." **(Arthur Koestler, author)**
❖ At one time the shadow of nuclear annihilation hung very heavily over people but now that threat seems to have receded. Do you think that people are still conscious of the danger or not? Should they be?

IN THE GLOSSARY ...

Arms Race; Nuclear Club.

9.4 PACIFISM

For the first three centuries of its existence few members of the Christian Church joined the Roman Army. They knew only too well the teaching of Jesus:

> "Blessed are the peacemakers;
> they shall be called God's children."
> (Matthew 5.9)

> "Do not resist those who wrong you. If anyone slaps you on the right cheek, turn and offer him the other also." (Matthew 5.39)

Then, when Constantine became a Christian, the Christian religion became the 'official' religion of the Roman Empire. Christians felt free to join the Army and many of them served in it in the years leading up to the collapse of the Roman Empire in 410 CE.

Suddenly, pacifism was out of fashion. Since then, it has never been the 'official' teaching of the Church.

What is Christian pacifism?

You do not need to be a Christian to be a pacifist. There are many people who believe that it is wrong to use violence in any situation yet they are not Christians. They simply cannot imagine any situation in which the use of violence can be morally justified. Christians who are pacifists justify their belief on Biblical grounds. In particular:

a) The straightforward commandment "Thou shalt not kill" (Exodus 20.13), which would seem to clearly outlaw killing in any situation. This includes every act of violence committed in war.

A *Why do you think the charge of cowardice was often levelled against pacifists in the First World War, even though their non-combatant duties often took them to the front line unarmed?*

b) The teaching of Jesus in the Sermon on the Mount recorded in Matthew 5-7. Among the many possible verses in support the Christian pacifist would point to:

❖ "Do not resist those who wrong you…" (5.39)
❖ "Love your enemies and pray for your persecutors…"(5.44)
❖ "There must be no limit to your goodness…" (5.48)

It is difficult to see how these verses could point to anything other than a pacifist approach to life.

c) The actions of Jesus as he was arrested (Luke 22.39-53). As Judas led the Roman soldiers to Jesus and identified him with a kiss one of his disciples, Peter, drew a sword. He cut off the ear of the High Priest's servant but Jesus stopped him with the words:

"Stop! No more of that!" (Luke 22.51)

Jesus then healed the ear of the servant before allowing himself to be arrested without a struggle.

Conscientious Objectors

In times of war many pacifists register as 'Conscientious Objectors'. This means they believe that they cannot take up arms and fight. The Roman Catholic Church, which does not have a strong tradition of pacifism, teaches its members that if they cannot fight they must offer themselves for other duties instead. In the First and Second World War, conscientious objectors often found themselves in the front line carrying out non-combatant duties such as ambulance driving, stretcher-carrying, etc.

Only one branch of the Christian Church has declared itself to be openly pacifist and that is the Quakers (the Society of Friends). This has been the case since the start of the movement, under George Fox, in the 17th century. Quakers argue that the way to bring an end to war is to appeal to that part of God which is found in everyone. While war destroys all that is beautiful and valuable in the world, Quakers are encouraged to bear their testimony throughout the world that God brings love, care and non-violence into every situation, no matter how serious it appears to be.

ANSWER IN YOUR BOOK …

1 What was the attitude of the early Christians towards war?

2 What biblical evidence is there to support pacifism?

3 What are 'Conscientious Objectors'?

READ AND DECIDE …

Here are two quotations from Christians putting forward opposite points of view about pacifism:

a) Francis Schaeffer: "I am not a pacifist because pacifism in this fallen world in which we live means that we desert the people who need our greatest help."

b) Dietrich Bonhoeffer: "The only way to overcome evil is to let it run itself to a standstill… Resistance merely creates further evil and adds fuel to the flames."

Which of these two opinions do you most agree with?

WHAT DO YOU THINK?

In 1660 Quakers handed the following 'Declaration' over to King Charles II:

"We utterly deny all outward wars and strife; and fightings with outward weapons, for any end, or under any pretence whatever; this is our testimony to the whole world. The Spirit of Christ by which we are guided is not changeable, so as once to command us from a thing as evil, and again to move unto it; and we certainly know, and testify to the world that the Spirit of Christ, which leads us into all truth, will never move us to fight and war against any man with outward weapons, neither for the Kingdom of Christ, nor for the kingdoms of this world."

a) What does the word 'pacifism' mean?

b) What is the 'testimony to the whole world' of the Society of Friends?

c) What does the testimony mean when it says 'The Spirit of Christ by which we are guided is not changeable'?

d) Which two 'causes' for which people have fought in the past are ruled out in this testimony?

IN THE GLOSSARY …

Constantine; Pacifism; Sermon on the Mount; Judas Iscariot; Peter; High Priest; Conscientious Objector; Quakers.

9.5 THE UNITED NATIONS

When the First World War ended in 1918 many of the politicians involved were determined that such a tragic waste of life should never occur again. In 1920 a group of nations combined to form the 'League of Nations'. The League had no army of its own and so could not enforce 'peace' anywhere. Instead, it relied simply on persuasion and negotiation. The U.S.A. never joined the League of Nations and Russia withdrew in 1939. It failed to prevent the outbreak of war in 1939 and finally folded in 1946.

The United Nations

By 1945 steps were being taken to form a new peace-keeping organisation. Representatives of 51 nations had already met in New York in the previous year to draw up a Charter for the 'United Nations'. The purposes of the new organisation were firmly laid out in the Preamble to the Charter:

a) To save succeeding generations from the scourge of war.
b) To reaffirm a faith in basic human rights.
c) To promote social progress and better standards of living throughout the world.
d) To unite and strengthen all member nations in order to maintain international peace and security.
e) To ensure that armed conflict was not used anywhere unless it was in the common interest.

How does the organisation work?

Member states send delegates to the U.N. to work towards achieving these aims. The organisation has a number of councils and agencies and among them are the following:

❖ *The General Council.* Every member country elects one representative to the General Assembly. It is here that most of the debates about world issues take place.
❖ *The Security Council.* This body exists to try to keep peace whenever it is threatened. Five countries – the U.S.A., Russia, the U.K., France and China – are permanent members of the Security Council while the other members of the U.N. take it in turns.
❖ *The Secretariat.* Under the Secretary-General the Secretariat is responsible for the day-by-day work of the U.N. It seeks to mediate in international disputes whilst carrying out the wishes of the U.N. itself.
❖ *The International Court of Justice.* This Court, which meets in the Hague in the Netherlands, tries to settle legal disputes between different countries.
❖ *The Food and Agricultural Organisation (FAO).* This is mainly concerned with world food supplies and agricultural development in Third World countries.
❖ *The World Health Organisation (WHO).* This organisation works throughout the world to combat disease and illness.
❖ *The International Childrens Emergency Fund (UNICEF).* This body concentrates on the needs of children throughout the world – especially the victims of war, epidemics, hunger and disease.

A *This irrigation project is just one of the many projects funded by the United Nations. Find out as much as you can about the different agencies of the U.N. and the work that they do.*

How effective is the U.N?

It is almost impossible to measure the effectiveness of an organisation like the U.N. Certainly, it has done a lot of excellent work in the areas of agriculture, health, education and disaster relief in the past. It has, however, been far less successful in preventing war and conflict.

Although there has not been a world conflict since the U.N. was set up in 1945 it has been powerless to halt many disputes in recent years. When it has intervened it has often made the situation worse. Those who are looking for reasons to criticise the U.N. need only point to places like Rwanda, Somalia, the Sudan, Bosnia and Chechyna.

B *Scenes like this are commonplace in today's world. The United Nations has failed many times recently in its attempts to solve problems between nations before they degenerate into war and bloodshed. Can you think of any effective way in which most wars could be prevented?*

ANSWER IN YOUR BOOK ...

1 Why was the United Nations set up in the first place?

2 What were the original aims of the United Nations and were they, in your opinion, realistic?

3 Outline the different ways in which the United Nations is organised.

WRITE AN ESSAY ...

Over the next few weeks watch the news and look in newspapers and magazines for items about the work of the United Nations. Make a folder on the work of the U.N. before writing between 500 and 600 words on the following essay title:

'The work of the United Nations in the modern world – why it is difficult but essential.'

USE YOUR IMAGINATION ...

Imagine that you have been given a brief by the nations of the world to prevent as many wars and conflicts as possible. You are allowed to follow any approach that you think will be effective and to set up any organisations which might be necessary. Describe how you would go about your work and how you think the world could be made a safer place for everyone.

10.1 WORLD POVERTY

As far as wealth and poverty are concerned the world can be divided into two clear sections:

1 The North or Developed World – sometimes called the 'First World'. This consists of those countries which enjoy a high standard of living and includes North America, Western Europe and Australasia.

2 The South or Developing World – sometimes called the 'Third World'. These are countries which have a much lower standard of living. Some Third World countries are very poor (Sudan, Somalia, Bangladesh, etc) while others are less so (Peru, Bolivia, Colombia, etc).

People sometimes talk of the 'Second World' as well. This refers mainly to countries in the old Communist Empire such as Russia, Romania and Hungary.

The Developing World

It is very important to distinguish between 'relative poverty' and 'absolute poverty'. There are parts of Great Britain which are poor compared with other parts of the country and this is called 'relative poverty'. Even the poorest parts of Great Britain, however, are rich compared with those parts of the Developing World which exist in 'absolute poverty'. Many countries in the Developing World have the following problems:

a) *A high level of malnutrition (Unit 10.2).* The difference in calorie intake between countries in the rich and poor parts of the world is truly astonishing. In the world's poorest countries 75% of the whole population (compared with just 6% in Britain) try to make a living out of agriculture. This is largely 'subsistence farming', with people just growing enough to

A *This school in Nepal is typical of many throughout the Developing World. Why do you think there is such a close connection between illiteracy and poverty?*

meet their own basic needs. They have little or none left over to sell so they have no money to buy those items which they cannot grow.

b) *A largely illiterate and uneducated population (Unit 10.3).* There is a direct link between the level of poverty and the rate of illiteracy. Those people who are illiterate in the world today (some 850,000,000 in total) can find no way out of the 'poverty trap'.

c) *A high level of disease and illness.* For people living in Developing Countries, life is full of obstacles. If they survive the perils of childbirth, they discover that their lifestyle leaves them open to all kinds of disease and illness. At least 25% of the world's population (some 1,500,000,000 people) cannot reach clean water. The nearest doctor or clinic is often several days walk away.

d) *A high rate of infant mortality.* Babies are at their most vulnerable in their first year of life. Of the 20,000,000 people who die as a result of malnutrition in the world each year, 75%

have yet to reach their 5th birthday. Malnourished mothers are unable to feed their underfed babies, creating a 'vicious circle'.

e) *A low life expectancy.* A person's life expectancy is the age that they can reasonably be expected to reach. In the U.K., men can expect to live until they are 73 and women until they are 77. In many Developing Countries the life expectancy is little more than 45 years.

The Brandt Report

In 1980 a group of political and economic experts drew up the 'Brandt Report'. This focussed everyone's attention on the enormous gap between the world's richest and poorest countries. The Report made the point that the developed countries of the North contain around 25% of the world's population and over 75% of the world's resources. The poor Southern countries have the impossible task of trying to feed 75% of the world's population (4,000,000,000 people) on less than 25% of the world's income.

Yet, as the Brandt Report emphasised, the economies of all the world's countries are dependent upon each other. The whole population of the world lives on the same planet and what happens in one part of the world affects the lives of people in countries thousands of miles away. The rich countries have a moral duty to help the poorer countries. It is also in their own long-term interests to do so.

B *This young child is dying from malnutrition. Try to find out what all people, children and adults, need to consume in the way of calories to remain healthy. How does the average calorie consumption in Developing Countries compare with that in Developed Countries?*

ANSWER IN YOUR BOOK ...

1 What do we mean when we speak of the First, Second and Third Worlds?

2 Can you explain what is meant by 'relative poverty' and 'absolute poverty'?

3 What was the Brandt Report and what did it have to say?

READ AND DECIDE ...

This quotation comes from the Brandt Report. Read it through carefully:

"Many hundreds of millions of people are preoccupied solely with survival and elementary needs. For them work is frequently not available or, when it is, pay is very low and conditions are often barely tolerable. Homes are constructed of impermeable (non-waterproof) materials and have neither piped water nor sanitation. Electricity is a luxury … Primary schools, where they exist, may be free and not too far away but children are needed for work and cannot easily be spared for schooling … Flood, drought or disease affecting people or livestock can destroy livelihoods without hope of compensation."

a) Rewrite the first sentence of this quotation, emphasising the point that the Report is making.

b) Which problems facing people who live in the Developing World are highlighted here?

c) Try to find out what is being done to help solve some of these problems by such organisations as the United Nations, Oxfam, CAFOD, Christian Aid, etc.

WHAT DO YOU THINK?

The Brandt Report made the simple point that the problem of world poverty will never be solved until the world's richest countries are willing to give some of their wealth to the much poorer countries. How do you think this could be done? Can you see it happening in your lifetime?

IN THE GLOSSARY ...

Developed World; Developing Country; First World; Second World; Third World; Subsistence Farming.

10.2 WORLD HUNGER

Many more people die in today's world from hunger (malnutrition) and related illnesses than from any other cause, including war. Malnutrition kills:

❖ one person every 1.5 seconds;
❖ 38 people every minute;
❖ 55,000 people every day;
❖ 20,000,000 people every year.

75% of the people who die are children under the age of 5.

The paradox of hunger

World hunger is a very complicated problem and there are many misunderstandings about it. Four 'myths', in particular, need to be examined:

a) *That there is not enough food to go around*. The simple truth is that there is more than enough food in the world to feed everyone. Every person in the world could comfortably be given 3000 calories a day instead of the 1700 on which millions have to survive. The problem is that most of the food is in the wrong place. As 750,000,000 people go to their beds hungry every night, Europe destroys 1,500,000 tonnes of food every year. The U.S.A., for example, contains only 6% of the world's population yet consumes, and wastes, 35% of the world's resources.

b) *That world hunger is caused by over-population*. It is true that the population of the world is exploding (see Unit 10.5) and that this will cause many problems in the future. It is also true that the population is generally increasing fastest in those countries with the most severe food problems. Yet, when you look at the problem in terms of population density (the number of people in a country per square kilometre), the situation looks rather different. While there are, on average, 98 people to every square kilometre in Western

> **A** *How do you think we get ourselves into the situation of destroying food when so many people are starving?*

Europe, the figure is just 18 in Africa. The problem is that in poorer countries much of the land is infertile (deserts, mountains, etc) and people cannot afford the technology to improve and farm it. As a result, overcrowded Western Europe is able to feed all its people while, in sparsely populated Africa, millions die from malnutrition.

B Find out anything that you can about a natural disaster which has occurred in recent months. In particular, try to discover how it affected the everyday lives of the people in the area.

c) *That starvation is the result of natural disasters (droughts, earthquakes, floods, etc).* Natural disasters do not only affect the Developing Countries. Take one example. A serious drought hit the mid-West of the U.S.A. in 1988 yet no one died. A similar drought in the Sudan or Burkina Faso would have killed thousands. Why the difference? The U.S.A. has mountains of grain stored and the transport to distribute it. It can also offer the technical and financial aid needed to help the farmers get back on their feet. Developing Countries have neither the surplus grain or the necessary transport. People are forced to eat their own seed corn, meaning that there may be no harvest for many years to come.

d) *That science will be able to cure world hunger.* In the 1960s scientists worked hard to produce new, higher yielding strains of wheat and rice. During the so-called 'Green Revolution' these were introduced into many Developing Countries. They brought some benefits but not the miraculous results that were hoped for.

The conclusion is inescapable. The human race has the means to tackle the problem of world hunger and malnutrition. To do so, however, would require the rich countries to eat, and waste, far less than they do at present. Without this happening millions will continue to die each year.

ANSWER IN YOUR BOOK ...

1 Can you explain why millions of people die each year from malnutrition when there is more than enough food in the world to feed everyone?

2 Can you explain why world hunger is not simply the result of there being too many mouths to feed?

3 Why do the Developed Countries manage to deal with the consequences of natural disasters so much better than the Developing ones?

READ AND DECIDE ...

Cardinal Basil Hume, leader of Britain's Catholic community, had this to say about the extent of food wastage:

"There is surely a moral imperative to bring sanity to this crazy and deadly situation, to restore human dignity, to promote development and the possibility of peace. We must look at ourselves and our lifestyles. We must examine and change the processes and structures of the world which at the moment promote division and ultimately bring death…"

a) Do you think that the situation in the world today is 'crazy and deadly'?

b) Do you agree that millions of people in today's world lack 'human dignity'? If so, what is necessary to restore that dignity?

c) How do you think we would have to change our 'lifestyles' in order for the situation of millions of people in today's world to be changed?

d) Do you detect a willingness on the part of many people to change or not?

IN THE GLOSSARY ...

Developing Country.

10.3 WORLD LITERACY

The real difference between the Developed and the Developing countries is illustrated as clearly in education as anywhere else. Here are two pieces of information worth looking at:

1 In the U.K., as in almost all First World countries, many children start nursery school at the age of three; stay at school until they are eighteen and then go on to university or some other form of further education. 1% of the population are illiterate, being unable to read or write.

2 In Developing Countries the situation is reversed. In many countries there is little formal education and the majority of the population are illiterate. For instance, only 31% of the Sudan, 25% of Saudi Arabia, 10% of Niger, 34% of Nigeria and 9% of Burkina Faso are literate. In an increasingly sophisticated world this is a crippling disadvantage.

In these countries almost all of the resources are used in the battle for survival. Faced with hunger, poverty, war, poor communications and continually failing crops it is hardly surprising that many countries do not make education a particularly high priority. After all, people do not die from lack of education!

Trying to help

The problem of world illiteracy is a massive one. At least 800 million people in today's world are totally or partially illiterate. In many countries some form of education is provided at primary level but few children go on to secondary education. In the poorest countries less than 25% of children continue their schooling beyond the age of 11.

The United Nation's Educational, Scientific and Cultural Organisation (UNESCO) spearheads the efforts to help poor countries improve their educational services. In order to carry out their work UNESCO, like all of the agencies of the United Nations, depends on the money that donor countries like the U.S.A. and the U.K. provide. Unfortunately, that money has decreased in recent years and the work of UNESCO has lost ground.

With this in mind, two new approaches have been tried:

a) People from poorer countries have been sent to the Developed Countries in order to train as doctors, nurses and teachers. The students have then returned to their home countries fully trained. In the past Britain has welcomed hundreds of overseas students. In recent years, however, the fees charged to such students have increased considerably and the numbers have gone down.

b) Many countries have taken great strides towards being able to help themselves. Very successful 'literacy drives' have been launched in recent years in Nicaragua and Cuba among others. Children and young people have been educated to a certain level and then sent out to teach those who are still illiterate. Often, they start with members of their own families. In Cuba this effort has raised the overall literacy level of the people to 98%.

A *Why do you think that high levels of poverty and illiteracy inevitably go hand in hand?*

B *A games lesson in an African school. If you belonged to this school what is the minimum that you would expect from your education?*

1 What are 'literacy' and 'illiteracy'?

2 Why do some countries with a high level of illiteracy seem to place little emphasis upon education?

3 What are the alternative approaches to the literacy problem?

CAN YOU EXPLAIN?

The chart below illustrates what has been called 'the vicious circle of illiteracy.' Look at it carefully and explain, in your own words, just what this phrase means.

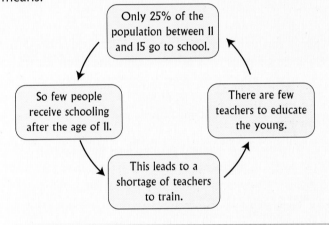

Only 25% of the population between 11 and 15 go to school.

So few people receive schooling after the age of 11.

There are few teachers to educate the young.

This leads to a shortage of teachers to train.

WHAT DO YOU THINK?

A missionary working on a literacy programme in North Africa has commented:

> "The measure of whether a country cares about its own people is the extent to which it is not only concerned to put food in its people's mouths, but also to build schools so that its people can receive an elementary education. Without such an education its people can do little to stave off the starvation which will inevitably come."

Explain, in about 500 words, why you think literacy is important.

IN THE GLOSSARY ...

Illiteracy; Developing Country; Literacy; Developed World.

10.4 NATURAL DISASTERS

Every year terrible natural disasters hit the headlines and we read accounts of thousands of people losing their lives or suffering. Christians and non-Christians alike have wondered for centuries why God allows suffering on such an immense scale.

Acts of God?

Insurance companies have described natural disasters as 'acts of God' for a long time. Why do many people still seem to regard them in this way?

1 In ancient times, people believed that spirits or gods lived in the earth, sky and sea. Each aspect of nature was ruled over by a separate deity. Sometimes the spirits or gods quarrelled and a natural disaster was the outcome. People offered gifts or sacrifices to the gods to try and appease them and so avoid such catastrophes.

2 While modern science provides us with so many answers it still seems powerless to prevent natural disasters from occurring, or even predict when and where they will happen. Whether we are talking of widespread flooding, earthquakes or drought, natural disasters seem to be chance occurrences.

3 Natural disasters underline the helplessness of humanity in the face of nature. People cannot even protect themselves, leave alone control the forces unleashed against them. Natural disasters remind us all that we are frail human beings.

The major problem about natural disasters is not so much that they happen. It is that they happen to a comparatively small group of people, usually in the Third World. When disaster strikes such countries do not have the resources or technology to launch an effective rescue or rebuilding operation. It often takes days for the rescue forces to reach the affected area. International organisations like Oxfam and the Red Cross play a vital part in launching appeals for clothing, housing, food and money.

Natural disasters do, of course, strike countries in the developed world as well. The difference lies in the impact they have and their response to them. Such countries usually have the resources readily available to minimise the devastation caused and look after those people who are affected.

A *Almost 4000 people died in an earthquake in Japan in 1995. What kind of questions do you think the people who survived might have asked?*

B   What do natural disasters teach us about ourselves?

How can God let this happen?

This is one of the hardest questions of all for Christians to answer. The dilemma is the same as that which Christians face over suffering. They believe that they worship a God of love. Yet if God is all-loving and all-powerful why does he allow these disasters to take place? Indeed, it was God who created a world in the first place in which such disasters are possible!

The Bible provides few answers. Those that it does provide would be questioned by most people today:

a) *That the world created by God was perfect.* The suffering in the world is the direct result of human sin. Most of it is caused by the forces of evil, the Devil. Natural disasters fall into this category. Clearly, some disasters may be caused by human interference with the natural forces but this does not apply to most tragedies.

b) *That natural disasters are sent by God to punish the evil.* This happened with the 'plagues' that fell on the Egyptians when they held the Israelites as captives (Exodus 9.23-25). Few people today, however, see the natural disaster as part of God's judgement on the world. The victims are usually some of the poorest people in the world who are far more sinned against than sinners.

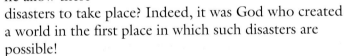

ANSWER IN YOUR BOOK ...

1 Why are natural disasters often called 'acts of God'?
2 What does it mean to call a natural disaster a 'chance occurrence'?
3 What answers does the Bible put forward to explain natural disasters?

WHAT DO YOU THINK?

a) Do you think that calling a natural disaster 'an act of God' helps people to come to terms with it? Could it be a way of avoiding the issue and not doing anything about the problem?

b) Do you think that natural disasters make it more difficult, or impossible, to believe in God?

c) Do you think there is any way in which some good could come from a natural disaster? If so, how?

FIND OUT AND NOTE ...

Collect as much information as you can about recent natural disasters? Could any blame be attached to anyone for any of the disasters? Would it have helped if such blame could have been apportioned?

IN THE GLOSSARY ...

Natural Disaster.

10.5 WORLD POPULATION

The greatest threat to the future survival of the human race is over-population. The simple statistics are these:

- ❖ every four seconds six babies are born;
- ❖ every minute 90 babies are born;
- ❖ every hour 5,400 babies are born;
- ❖ every day 130,000 babies are born.

The consequence of so many babies being born is catastrophic. The population of the world increases by more than the population of the United Kingdom (55.3 million) every year. Now the population of the world is doubling every 35 years. By the year 2000 it is certain to have reached 6000 million compared with about 1600 million in 1900. Little wonder that this increase has been described as an 'explosion'.

Where do all these people live? About 50% of the world's population now live in cities. In 1960 there were 100 cities with a population of more than 1,000,000 people. By the year 2000 there will be over 500 such cities. The largest of these, Mexico City, currently has a population of about 15,000,000.

The Problems of Population Growth

The population of the world is not increasing at the same rate everywhere. In some developed countries – such as Norway, Sweden and Switzerland – population growth is virtually at a standstill and this is causing some concern. Their problem is simply this. In years to come there will be more and more old people in the population and fewer of working age to support them.

Compare this with many developing countries where the population is increasing very rapidly. In Kenya, for example, the population increases by some 8% each year and this is also true of many other African countries. The latest figures available suggest that 1 in every 4 people in the world today are Chinese. The population is also increasing very quickly in most South American countries. As the 'infant mortality' rate is very high in

A Why do you think that the population problem has been described as the greatest threat confronting mankind? What kind of problems accompany an ever-increasing number of people?

these countries and many hands are necessary to work the fields, large families are seen as being some kind of 'insurance policy'. They also guarantee that people will be looked after when they reach old age. This is an essential precaution in countries which do not have a social security system or an old age pension.

The population explosion causes many problems worldwide:

a) It causes a housing problem. Millions of people are without homes of any kind while much of the housing that does exist lacks basic amenities.

b) It leads to an increase in the number of large cities. Not only are these cities built on valuable land but they also generate a whole variety of social problems including violence and crime, drug-trafficking, etc.

c) It makes the world hunger problem even more difficult to solve.

d) It leads to the increased production of human waste which is now polluting to the world's oceans, rivers and skies.

Attempts so far to slow down the population explosion have failed. India, for example, with a total population of 625,000,000, tried a mass sterilisation and contraception programme. Men were rewarded with a cow, a much valued possession, if they came forward to be sterilised. Women received a radio if they had a contraceptive device fitted. The campaign lasted for five years but it was a failure. In China the government has imposed a strict 'one child' policy. Most second, and subsequent, pregnancies are aborted. If a couple do have a second child they face heavy tax penalties. Despite these restrictions the population of China continues to grow rapidly.

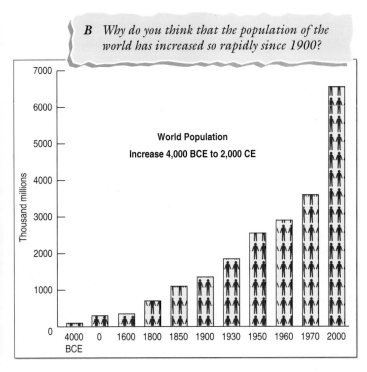

B Why do you think that the population of the world has increased so rapidly since 1900?

World Population
Increase 4,000 BCE to 2,000 CE

Thousand millions

7000 — 6000 — 5000 — 4000 — 3000 — 2000 — 1000 — 0

4000 BCE | 0 | 1600 | 1800 | 1850 | 1900 | 1930 | 1950 | 1960 | 1970 | 2000

ANSWER IN YOUR BOOK ...

1 What is meant by the 'population explosion'?
2 How has the population of the world grown across different countries?
3 What problems are being caused by the population explosion?

WHAT DO YOU THINK?

a) Why do you think that the birth-control programme in India was unsuccessful?

b) Do you think it is right:
  ❖ for a government to try to bribe people to have fewer children?
  ❖ for a government to force people to have fewer children?

Give as many reasons as possible for your answers.

c) Can you think of any alternative solutions to the population explosion in the developing world?

DISCUSS AMONG YOURSELVES...

These are three opinions expressed by young people concerning the problem of over-population. Decide what you think about them:

a) "No wonder people in the developing world have problems – they have too many children. If you ask me, compulsory sterilisation is the only answer."

b) "The Roman Catholic Church is right when it insists that the answer is not birth-control but the alleviation of poverty. People would not have so many children if they did not have to worry about their babies dying or how they were going to be looked after in old age."

c) "People should be left free to have as many children as they want. No one, not even their government, has the right to tell them how many babies to have. That is personal to each and every couple."

IN THE GLOSSARY ...

Population Explosion; Developed World; Developing Country; Infant Mortality Rate; Sterilisation; Contraception.

10.6 GOD, THE EARTH AND THE HUMAN RACE

Christians should be at the forefront of those working to conserve the planet on which we live. Along with Jews and Muslims they strongly believe that this world was created by God. They believe that the world did not come into existence purely by accident. It was planned by God and filled with divine purpose and goodness.

Divine Creation

This idea of divine creation is reflected very strongly in the Old Testament. Here is just one quotation from the Psalms:

> "To the Lord (God)
> belongs the earth and
> everything in it,
> the world and all its
> inhabitants.
> For it was he who founded it
> on the seas
> and planted it firm on the
> waters beneath."
> (Psalm 24.1,2)

The prophets of Israel continually told the people that God had created the earth and then entrusted to men and women the responsibility of looking after it. The human race is answerable to God for everything that it does and this includes its relationship to the earth. In Psalm 8 we are told precisely what this can mean:

a) When the Psalmist looks at the heavens, the moon and the stars he is struck by his own impotence and frailty.

b) Yet God in his wisdom has given the human race authority and power over everything that he has made. As the Psalmist states:

> "You make him master over all that you have made…"(v.6)

A *Many people believe that humanity should replace everything that it takes out of the earth. Do you think that this would be a good idea?*

This kind of authority is open to all kinds of abuse. Desmond Morris, the well-known anthropologist, had some very strong words to say about the idea that the human race is the master of all things. He said the following:

> "Who is to blame for the crisis we face? First and foremost, I accuse the religious leaders of the world. They have fed mankind with the dangerous myth that humanity is somehow above nature, and that it is our God-given right to hold dominion over the earth and subdue it … they are a disgrace."

B *Do you think that men are the masters of all things? Do you think that the crisis over the environment would have been prevented if women, rather than men, had been taking the most important decisions?*

It is the word 'dominion', found in Genesis 1.28, which has caused so many problems. Regrettably, it has been taken by many Christians in the past to mean 'domination'. They have taught the people that human beings are free to use the whole of nature for their own ends. Desmond Morris is quite right. It is a disgrace. Other religious traditions, especially Hinduism and the religions of the native North Americans, have had much more to say about the need to respect the earth than has Christianity. Chief Seattle, a 19th century leader of the Suqaumish Indians, told the whole of America to:

> "Teach your children what we have taught our children, that the earth is our mother. Whatever befalls the earth befalls the children of the earth…"

You can find the whole of this quotation in **READ AND DECIDE…**

Yet the notion of 'domination' is not the only Christian word on this subject. There are two quite different stories (myths) about the creation of the world in Genesis. The first certainly places humanity at the summit of God's creation but the second, in Genesis 2, sees things in a rather different light. We read:

> "The Lord God took the man and put him in the Garden of Eden to till it and look after it." (Genesis 2.15)

The task given to man is to look after creation as a 'steward', knowing that he is answerable to God. This line of approach has come down from the teaching of St Francis of Assissi to the present time.

ANSWER IN YOUR BOOK …

1 What do Christians, Jews and Muslims believe about the world?

2 What is the significance of the two accounts of creation in the Book of Genesis?

3 How would you explain the difference between 'dominion' and 'domination'?

READ AND DECIDE …

Through their religion and way of life the Indians in North America have always expressed the unity between the earth and the human race. Chief Seattle is the most well-known exponent of this unity. When the Americans were trying to negotiate with him over the transfer of some land he told them:

> "Teach your children what we have taught our children, that the earth is our mother. Whatever befalls the earth befalls the children of the earth. If we spit on the ground we spit on ourselves. This we know. The earth does not belong to us; we belong to the earth… The earth is precious to God and to harm the earth is to heap contempt on the Creator."

a) Why do you think that the earth is called 'our mother' by Chief Seattle? What do you think he was trying to tell the American people?

b) What do you think he meant when he said: "The earth does not belong to us; we belong to the earth…"

c) How do you think the attitude of Chief Seattle towards the earth differs from that held by most people? What difference would it make if his attitude was adopted by everyone?

IN THE GLOSSARY …

Old Testament; Psalms; Prophet; Genesis.

10.7 POLLUTION (1)

Considerable scientific achievements in recent years have enabled us to look back on planet earth from the outer reaches of space. One of the most important lessons that we have learnt since space exploration began is that we all live in a 'global village'. This means that something which takes place thousands of miles away can affect all of us on earth. This came home powerfully to everyone with the explosion at the nuclear power plant in Chernobyl in the old U.S.S.R. The radioactive fallout from that particular catastrophe reached Britain only a few weeks later.

Way open for cuts in greenhouse gases

Choking on the very air we breathe

Holiday alert as smog level hits danger point

Smog shrou over nation recalls the filthy Fiftie

Arctic trees show signs of life as temperatures rise

Way cleared towards greenhouse gas targets

Blooms 'herald global

Action needed to save 600 species

Oil producers threaten global warming summit

Three cities exceed EC limits on air pollution

£1m campaign to reduce need for abortions

Seaside bathers 'face high risk of viral illness'

Gummer orders fish study after US warming alert

Medical waste

Quality of life falling

British beaches 'still filthy' despite £9 billion clean-up

Cyanide kills 5,000 fish   Mankind doomed   in 'next few years'

Soaring smog levels may kill 10,000 people a year

A *What do you think are the main causes of pollution in today's world?*

We have also learned something else. The news about the state of planet earth from outer space is far from good. Pictures have shown us the extent to which we are polluting the atmosphere by our activities on earth. We have also been able to monitor the 'global warming' which is taking place. Satellite pictures of the holes in the Ozone Layer tell their own story.

In this chapter we will look at three aspects of the pollution of the earth which are causing particular concern.

Global warming

Our planet is surrounded by a blanket of gases which insulate it and guarantee a temperature which is able to sustain life. Without this blanket the earth would be little more than a floating rock in space, too cold to maintain life. The blanket, then, acts like a kind of greenhouse around the earth but, through pollution, the greenhouse is becoming too warm.

During the past 100 years the overall temperature of the earth's surface has risen by about ½%. That doesn't sound much until you realise that if the temperature was to rise by just 1½% ice-caps in the Arctic and

Antarctic would melt and the waters of the oceans would rise by 1½ metres, with catastrophic consequences. Many low-lying areas in the world would simply be over-run by sea-water.

The Ozone Layer

Between 6 and 30 miles above our heads a small percentage of oxygen in the atmosphere is made into ozone. This ozone forms a layer which absorbs the lethal ultra-violet rays from the sun. Without this layer, people on earth would be vulnerable to a whole range of hazards from skin cancer and eye cataracts to crop damage. This ozone layer, however, is now being damaged. The main causes of this

B *Why are rainforests so important for the future well-being of both the human race and the planet?*

are chlorine compounds, such as CFCs, which remain active in the atmosphere for up to 100 years. Although these are now being phased out of aerosol cans they are still present in old refrigerators and other pieces of machinery. The worrying fact is that the present holes in the ozone layer will take at least a century to repair themselves after the offending chemicals have been removed from the atmosphere – and that hasn't even happened yet!

The Tropical Rainforests

Rainforests form a truly astonishing part of our environment. They are important because 75% of all species, most of which have not yet even been named, are found in the rainforests. The destruction of the rainforests is taking place at a truly astonishing rate. The following has been said about this matter:

> "It is as though the nations of the world decided to burn their libraries without bothering to see what is in them."

We do know that the rainforests have provided the raw materials for many of our most important drugs including reserpine, which is widely used to control high blood pressure. The United Nations inform us that a rainforest area the size of England and Wales is disappearing each year. Over 50% of the rainforests which existed in the 1970s have now been destroyed. The results of this are far-reaching. Rainforests are

essential for regulating the climate and controlling flooding. In one case, flooding in Thailand claimed 450 lives after deforestation and caused £200,000,000 worth of damage.

As we shall see in Unit 10.8 this pollution also takes place on a more local level, with equally disastrous consequences for the environment.

ANSWER IN YOUR BOOK ...

1 What is global warming and why does it present such a great challenge to humanity?

2 Why is the ozone layer so important to the future of mankind?

3 Why should the widespread destruction of the world's rainforests be a great cause for alarm?

READ AND DECIDE ...

The Bible does not appear to have much to say about the need to care for the planet. You might, however, be able to learn quite a lot by simply reading between the lines. Look up these references and answer the questions.

a) **Genesis 1.9-19; 20-31; 2.15-18**
Is there any noticeable difference in these two accounts of humanity's place in creation?

b) **Isaiah 32.15-17**
This speaks of the wilderness becoming fruitful but only after something else happens. What is that?

c) **Leviticus 21.23-25; 19.9,10**
Do these pieces of advice have anything to say about the way that we treat the earth today?

WHAT DO YOU THINK?

Abbess Hildegarde of Bingen, who lived in the 12th century, had this to say:
> "All of creation God gives to humankind to use. If this privilege is misused, God's justice permits creation to punish humanity."

a) Can you rewrite this quotation to fully bring out its meaning?

b) Can you find any examples from the news recently to show that nature is perfectly capable of 'hitting back' at the human race?

IN THE GLOSSARY ...

Global Warming; Ozone Layer; United Nations.

10.8 POLLUTION (2)

The greatest threat to the environment is the way that each one of us lives. Our 'throw-away' lifestyle creates great mountains of waste. The cars that we use cause considerable pollution. Our farming in the last few decades has polluted the earth and destroyed hundreds of miles of hedgerows and industry is allowed to pollute rivers and streams by dumping its waste products. Let us look at some of the aspects of pollution in Britain more closely:

a) *The loss of habitats.* Since the Second World War Britain has lost:

❖ 145,000 miles of hedgerows;
❖ 95% of its wildflower meadows;
❖ 50% of its ancient woodlands.

These habitats are 'home' to numerous species of plants, animals and insects. Destroy the habitat and you are probably destroying the species as well.

A It is estimated that by the year 2025 the number of vehicles on Britain's roads will double. Worldwide there are now 400 million motor-cars, not to mention lorries and coaches. Can you come up with any ideas as to how society can deal with the motor-car without destroying the environment?

b) *Air and water pollution.* Nitrates and pesticides have been allowed to run off farmland to pollute local streams and rivers. About 4,000,000 people in the U.K. receive substandard water and some of Britain's most important buildings, such as St Paul's in London, are being eaten away by acid rain (rain that is so polluted that it has become acidic). Car emissions (apart from the 50% which are lead-free) put a neuro-toxin in the atmosphere which lowers the intelligence level of children and affects their behaviour. Many cities in the U.K. are now thinking of banning the car from city-centres when pollution reaches a certain limit.

B The volume of goods that are packaged in the U.K. has trebled in the last twenty years. Why do you think this has happened and what do you think we can do about it?

148

c) *Waste.* The average household in Britain disposes of a tonne of rubbish each year. This includes:

- ❖ 100 bottles or jars;
- ❖ 70 food cans;
- ❖ 100 pounds of plastic;
- ❖ 300 pounds of food waste.

The waste must be put somewhere with landfill sites usually being used. Yet such sites can be dangerous. It is thought that 1300 of them in the U.K. alone are in danger of polluting the local water supply while 1000 are emitting the greenhouse gas, methane. Recycling is the most sensible option and this idea is gradually catching on with the British public. Some 30% of British waste paper is now recycled compared with 15% in the 1970s. We will discuss recycling further in Unit 10.9.

d) *Energy.* In the 1950s nuclear energy was seen as the great hope for the future but this is no longer the case. Chernobyl has warned us of the danger of nuclear energy while we have learnt the hard way about the problems of disposing of nuclear waste. We now face a problem in that more conventional sources of energy (coal, electricity) are set to run out in the not too distant future.

Obviously, society cannot continue to rush headlong down this path which will lead eventually to destruction. The whole of the world's fragile future depends upon a fine balance being maintained between the planet and humanity. Part of the answer lies in the willingness of the human race to adjust its lifestyle and change its attitudes. As Mahatma Gandhi once said:

> "There is enough for every man's need but not for every man's greed."

However, more than this is needed. Governments and large multi-national companies need to change the way that they approach the environment. At the moment they are simply concerned about squeezing as much profit out of the earth as possible. So much is taken out yet so little is put back in. If we continue along this path the end of this planet, and the end of the human race, is guaranteed. The only question then becomes 'When'?

ANSWER IN YOUR BOOK ...

1 The motor-car has been described as one of the greatest curses of the 20th century. What do you think was meant by this?

2 Why is waste disposal such a problem in the world today?

3 What has to be done if the human race is to have any kind of a future?

DISCUSS AMONG YOURSELVES...

Here are four opinions for you to think over, discuss and draw your own conclusions about:

a) Lester Brown, American environmentalist:
"We have not inherited the earth from our fathers, we are borrowing it from our children."

b) Jacques Cousteau, underwater explorer:
"If human civilisation is going to invade the waters of the earth, then let it be first of all to carry a message of respect – respect for all life."

c) Albert Schweitzer, African missionary:
"Until he extends the circle of his compassion to all living things, man will not himself find peace."

d) Motto of Christian Lifestyle Movement:
"Live more simply that others may simply live."

10.9 CONSERVATION

A few years ago a book was written with the title '1000 Days to save the Planet'. This time-limit has now passed and the planet is still here. The title was alarmist. This does not mean, however, that all is well. It isn't. Unless urgent action is taken, there is no guarantee that the universes will have a long-term future. This is why 'conservation' is so vitally important. Whatever mistakes the human race has made in the past, and there have been many, it must take active, and drastic steps, both in the present and future. Among them must be the following:

a) *Waste must be dealt with.* Some 90% of all household rubbish ends up on landfill sites yet 70% of rubbish in dustbins could be recycled. Only 30% of all newspapers and magazines are recycled yet trees are continually chopped down to provide paper. Most people have recycling facilities close by but comparatively few use them. Environmentally friendly products are available in many areas of life if people would only use them. Industries must be forced to find other ways of disposing of their waste. No one should be allowed to use local streams or rivers for this purpose. A large question mark should be placed over the use of nuclear power since no safe way has been found of disposing of nuclear waste. The practice of dumping such waste in Third World countries and in the oceans should be stopped.

b) *Energy must be conserved.* Both the planet and the individual benefit if energy is conserved. Houses should be insulated to prevent energy loss and all household appliances should be tested for energy efficiency. Unnecessary car journeys should be eliminated and car-sharing made a regular practice. This would greatly reduce the amount of pollution that is released into the atmosphere.

c) *Pollution must be tackled.* Many household products, such as washing powder and bleach, have a detrimental effect on the environment. Some 50% of the pollution in the atmosphere is caused by 10% of the cars on the road and if this problem were tackled it would go some way towards dealing with the twin evils of global warming and the destruction of the ozone layer. The use of pesticides on the land is a crucial issue and the move towards eating organic food is also important. A great deal of money needs to be spent on dealing with the problem of human sewage, since this is dumped into the sea. Of 365 beaches in Britain surveyed in a recent European Community investigation, only 27 came up to standard. The rest were contaminated

A *Is it just ignorance that prevents people from attempting to recycle much of their rubbish?*

by raw sewage, not only posing a real threat to human beings bathing in the water but also destroying many of the fish and other marine life that live in it.

d) *Nature must be allowed to grow naturally.* Problems such as the destruction of the world's most important habitats, like rainforests, need to be tackled urgently. Once these places have been destroyed they cannot be replaced and the destruction of the planet will draw closer. On a more local level the growth of wildlife gardens and the replacement of miles of hedgerows are essential. Many wildlife species are now close to extinction because their sources of food and shelter have been taken away.

An encouraging sign is that many companies now undertake a 'green audit'. Among the questions that are asked are the following:

B *An almost continuous layer of pollution sits over this town. How do you think such pollution affects the health of the city's inhabitants?*

❖ Whether the company uses many disposable products and, if so, what happens to them?
❖ Whether the company tries to buy green products and makes use of recycling facilities?
❖ Whether any use is made of toxic products and, if so, how the environment and workers are protected from them?
❖ Whether steps are in place to conserve as much energy as possible?

ANSWER IN YOUR BOOK ...

1 What is 'recycling'?
2 Why is it essential to tackle pollution on our beaches and in our seas?
3 What is a Company 'green audit'?

FIND OUT AND NOTE ...

There are many charities in the U.K. which seek to help the environment in some way. There may be a local one in your area? If so, find out as much as you can about it. Here are three organisations which work on both a national and international level to protect the environment. Find out as much as you can about the work that they do:

a) Friends of the Earth, U.K.
b) Council for the Protection of Rural England
c) Greenpeace

WHAT DO YOU THINK?

a) Why do you think that comparatively few people use the recycling facilities that have been provided?
b) Why do you think that rich countries often dump their most hazardous waste in Third World Countries?
c) Why do you think that tackling the excessive use of the motor-car is such an important environmental issue?

IN THE GLOSSARY ...

Landfill Site; Recycling.

THE GLOSSARY

A

Abortion – an operation carried out to remove the foetus from its mother's womb so that it can be destroyed.

Adolescence – the period between the ages of 13 and 18.

Adultery – a sexual relationship between a married person and someone to whom they are not married.

AID – (Artificial Insemination by Donor) – this takes place when sperm from an anonymous donor is implanted in a woman's body so that it can fertilise one of her eggs.

AIDS – a fatal disease brought on by the exchange of body fluids between two people.

AIH – (Artificial Insemination by Husband) – this takes place when a husband's sperm is implanted in his wife's body so that her egg can be fertilised.

Alcoholic – a man or a woman whose body has become addicted to alcohol.

Anglican Church – the name given to the Church of England in other countries outside of England.

Anti-semitism – any hatred or prejudice directed towards a person because he or she is a Jew.

Apartheid – (separate development of the races) – the policy adopted by the South African government between 1948 and 1994.

Archbishop of Canterbury – a clergyman appointed by the Prime Minister to lead the Church of England.

Arms Race – the practice of the major countries of the world since the Second World War in spending huge amounts of money to develop better arms and to sell many of them to other countries.

Automation – this takes place in industry when machines are used to do work which was previously done by human beings.

B

Bartering – an early system of exchanging goods and services rather than paying money.

Bible – the holy book for all Christians which is divided into the Old and New Testament.

Birth-control – any effective means of trying to limit the number of babies born.

Bisexuals – men and women who have sexual relationships with members of both sexes.

Bye-law – a law passed by a local council which only operates in its designated area.

C

Celibacy – the acceptance of the unmarried state as a gift from God.

Chastity – the practice of abstaining from sexual relationships, usually for religious reasons.

Church – the whole community of Christians throughout the world.

Civil War – an internal war usually involving government forces fighting opposition from within their own country.

Conception – the moment when a man's sperm fertilises a woman's egg (ovum) after sexual intercourse.

Condom – the most popular form of contraception. This involves a thin latex sheath being stretched over a man's erect penis.

Conscientious Objector – someone who refuses to fight in a war on moral or religious grounds.

Constantine (247-337 CE) – the Roman Emperor who converted to the Christian faith and declared Christianity to be a 'tolerated' religion throughout the Empire.

Contraception – any effective means used to prevent the conception of a baby taking place.

Crusades – the military enterprises in the 11th, 12th and 13th centuries in which Christian armies tried to conquer Palestine and release the city of Jerusalem from the Turks.

D

Developed World – the part of the world made up of the rich countries which have a highly developed and industrialised way of life.

Developing Country – a country which has a very low standard of living, relying mainly on agriculture.

Devil – (Satan) – the leader of those forces of evil which wage a constant war against God.

Drug Abuse – this happens every time a person uses unprescribed drugs for non-medical reasons.

Drug Addiction – this happens when a person's body suffers severe side-effects when a drug is withdrawn.

Drug Dependency – this happens whenever a person has become physically or psychologically dependent on a drug.

E

Embryo – the name given to a newly conceived baby for the first few weeks of its life.

Euthanasia – (easy-death) – the right for people to have their lives ended prematurely to save them from unnecessary suffering.

Extended Family – a family in which several generations live close together and depend heavily upon each other.

F

Fallopian Tubes – the tubes in a woman's body along which the egg travels each month on its way to the womb (uterus).

Family Planning – this takes place when a couple use contraception to plan the size of their family. It is also used to plan when each baby will be born.

First World – an alternative term for the Developed World.

Foetus – the name given to the embryo after about ten weeks of pregnancy.

G

Genesis – the first book in the Christian Bible, giving accounts of the creation of the world and the beginning of the Jewish people.

Genocide – the attempt by one nation to wipe out another nation, or group of people, completely.

Gentile – anyone who is not a Jew.

Global Warming – the process by which the planet is gradually getting warmer due to pollution.

Gospels – the books in the New Testament (Matthew, Mark, Luke and John) which tell the story of Jesus.

H

Hebrews – the early descendants of Abraham before they were called Jews.

Hermit – someone who seeks to devote their whole life to God by living alone in a deserted place.

Heterosexual – someone who is sexually attracted to members of the opposite sex.

High Priest – the leader of the Jews at the time of Jesus.

HIV – the virus which people contract through sexual intercourse and which usually leads to AIDS.

Holocaust – (wholly burnt offering) – the word used to describe the massacre of six million Jews by the Nazis in the Second World War.

Holy Communion – the most important service in the Christian Church where worshippers remember the death of Jesus through eating bread and drinking wine together.

Holy Scriptures – a descriptive term for the Bible.

Holy War – a conflict which is conducted in the name of God.

Homophobia – the common fear that some people have of homosexuals and homosexuality.

Homosexual – somebody who finds that they are sexually attracted to members of their own, and not the opposite, sex.

Hospice Movement – a system of care which offers people who are dying real control over their pain and a dignified death.

I

Illiteracy – the state of being unable to read or write.

Immigrant – someone who leaves their country of birth and settles in another country to live.

Infant Mortality Rate – the number of babies in every thousand that die before they reach their first birthday.

Infertility – a condition which can affect either men or women and means that they are unable to father or mother a child.

IVF – one of the answers to infertility, relying on the conception of a baby outside the body of the mother.

J

Jew – a person who is descended from one of the tribes of Judah although they may not practice the religion of Judaism.

John The Baptist – the cousin of Jesus who, according to the Gospels, was sent by God to prepare the people for the coming of Christ.

Judas Iscariot – one of the original disciples of Jesus who betrayed him to the Roman authorities.

Just War – a war which is considered to be justified as long as it is fought according to certain conditions.

Juvenile Delinquent – anyone convicted of breaking the law who is under the age of 19.

L

Landfill Site – an area which the local council provides for people to dump their rubbish.

Lesbianism – taking its name from a Greek island in the 7th century CE, lesbianism refers to homosexual activity among women.

Liberation Theology – the Christian ethic, developed in South America, which compels the Church to stand up for the poor, using violence if necessary.

Literacy – the skill to read and write.

M

Mass Media – a term used to describe all means of mass communication – television, newspapers, films, etc.

Materialism – an outlook on life which teaches that only the 'material' things of life matter and that there is no such thing as a spiritual dimension.

Methodist Church – a Protestant Church which came into being after the death of John Wesley (1703-91), an Anglican clergyman, and which is based on his teaching.

Missionary – (someone who is sent) – a man or a woman commissioned by a Christian community to carry the Christian Gospel to others, usually overseas.

Monk – a man who has dedicated himself to seeking God through a life of prayer and discipline and who lives in a monastery.

Monogamy – the practice followed in almost all societies of allowing a person to only be married to one person.

Moses – the leader and law-giver of the Israelites.

Muslim – (submission to God) – someone who is committed to the teachings of Islam.

N

Natural Disaster – a natural occurrence over which human beings have little, or no, control.

Nazarite Vow – a vow taken by men in Biblical times in which they dedicated themselves to God. They demonstrated this by not cutting their hair, drinking alcohol or having sexual relations.

New Testament – the second part of the Bible containing the Gospels and letters sent to the various Christian communities.

Nuclear Club – the term used to describe those countries in the world which possess nuclear weapons.

Nuclear Family – the modern arrangement where just two generations, parents and children, live together.

Nun – a woman who has committed herself to seeking God through prayer and discipline and who lives in a convent.

O

Old Testament – the books in the Bible which the Christian Church took over from the Jews.

One-parent Family – a family which is being brought up by just one parent, usually the mother.

Ozone Layer – the protective layer of gases around the planet which prevent harmful ultra-violet rays from reaching the earth.

P

Pacifism – the belief that all forms of violence are wrong.

Paul – the dedicated opponent of the Christian Church who was converted on the road to Damascus before becoming its most important leader and writer in the first century.

Peter – emerged from among the disciples of Jesus to become the leader of the early Christian Church and, according to the Roman Catholic Church, the first Pope.

Pledge – a popular tradition in Methodist circles in the 19th and early 20th centuries by which people promised that they would not drink any alcohol. This has also been common practice in Southern Ireland for many years.

Polygamy – the practice in a few societies of allowing a man to have more than one wife.

Pope – (Bishop of Rome) – the leader of the world's Roman Catholics.

Population Explosion – this refers to the fact that the population of the world has increased very rapidly (exploded) in recent decades.

Priest – a man or a woman who has been ordained by a bishop and authorised to administer the Sacraments.

Priesthood – this contains the ordained clergy of the Catholic Church who alone are authorised to administer the sacraments.

Primary Relationships – the most important relationships in our lives – e.g: those between parents and children, husbands and wives, etc.

Prisoner of Conscience – someone who is imprisoned, or tortured, because of their beliefs.

Probation – a form of punishment which can be imposed by a Court, curtailing a person's liberty by compelling them to report regularly to a Probation Officer.

Promiscuity – casual sexual behaviour.

Promised Land – (Canaan) – the country promised by God to the Israelites (Jews) when they were only a small and insignificant group of people.

Prophet – a man or woman who is called by God to pass on the divine message.

Protestant – any member of the Christian Church who does not belong to either the Roman Catholic or Orthodox Churches.

Psalms – a book in the Old Testament which is made up of songs or poems designed to be sung in worship.

Puberty – the changes which take place in a young person's body during adolescence.

Q

Quakers – (Society of Friends) – a denomination which arose in 17th century England because of the teaching of George Fox.

R

Racial Discrimination – this takes place whenever a person is discriminated against (disadvantaged) because of their skin colour.

Racial Prejudice – the attitude of mind which looks upon people as inferior if the colour of their skin is different.

Recidivist – someone who serves more than one sentence in prison.

Recycling – the process of re-using materials and goods in an environmentally friendly way.

Redundancy – money offered when people lose their employment.

Refugee – a person who has lost their home, usually because of war.

Retirement Pension – this is paid to a man in the U.K. when he reaches the age of 65 and a woman when she reaches 60 and stops working.

Roman Catholic Church – the community of Christians which owes its allegiance to the Pope as the successor of St Peter on earth.

S

Sabbath Day – the Jewish day of rest on the 7th day of the week.

Salvation Army – a Protestant organisation which was founded by William and Catherine Booth in 1880.

Satan – (The Accuser) – the leader of the evil spirits who oppose God in Christian belief.

Second Vatican Council – a Roman Catholic Council held in the early 1960s to bring its worship into line with the 20th century.

Second World – a term sometimes used to describe the old Communist countries of Eastern Europe.

Secondary Relationships – those relationships which do not play a major part in our lives.

Segregation – the policy practised by the South African Government under apartheid of keeping the different races in the country totally separated.

Separation – a period which most couples go through of living apart from each other before they divorce.

Sermon on the Mount – the most important collection of sayings and teachings of Jesus found in Matthew chapters 5 to 7.

Sexual Discrimination – a form of discrimination which takes place whenever a person is at a disadvantage because of their sex.

Sexually Transmitted Diseases – diseases which are passed on from one person to another through sexual intercourse.

Socialisation – the process by which an individual becomes ready to play their part in the society in which they live.

Soul – (spirit) – that part of the human personality which cannot be explained simply in terms of a person's physical characteristics.

Spouse – a person's husband or wife.

Stereotyping – a process by which certain characteristics are assumed common of all people who belong to a particular group.

Sterilisation – an operation which prevents a man or a woman from having any further children.

Subsistence Farming – the common practice in developing countries where a family only grows enough food to feed itself, without being able to sell a surplus.

Substance Abuse – this takes place whenever someone uses a substance (drug) for a purpose for which it was never intended.

Surrogacy – this takes place when a woman agrees to have a baby on behalf of someone else.

Synagogue – a Jewish place of worship.

T

Tee totaller – a person who does not drink any alcohol.

Temperance Movement – a movement among Nonconformist Churches in the 19th century which sought to persuade members not to drink any alcohol.

Ten Commandments – at the heart of the Torah, the Ten Commandments laid down a person's responsibilities to God and to his or her fellow human beings.

Terminal Illness – an illness in which a person has only a short amount of time to live.

Third World – a term for the Developing World.

Torah – the law which God gave to Moses on Mount Sinai.

U

United Nations – an organisation set up at the end of the Second World War with the aim of preventing future wars.

Uterus – (womb) – the place in a woman's body where the fertilised egg implants itself and grows into a baby.

V

Vegetarian – someone who does not eat meat or any meat products.

Virgin – someone who has never had sexual intercourse.

Vows – the promises which a man and a woman make to each other at their wedding service.

SOME USEFUL ADDRESSES

UNIT ONE – CLOSE TO HOME

- **Family Welfare Association.** 501/505, Kingsland Rd, Dalston E8 4AU
- **Gingerbread (For One-Parent Families).** 35, Wellington St, London WC2E 7BN
- **The Mother's Union.** Mary Summer House, 24, Tufton St, London SW1P 3RB
- **National Council for One-Parent Families.** 255, Kentish Town Rd, London NW5 2LX

UNIT TWO – MARRIAGE AND SEX

- **Campaign for Homosexual Equality.** PO Box 342, London WX1X ODU
- **Catholic Marriage Advisory Council.** 15, Lansdowne Rd, Holland Park, London W11 3AJ
- **Gay Christian Movement.** BM 6914, London WC1N 3XX
- **Health Education Service.** Hamilton House, Mabledon Place, London WC1H 9TX
- **RELATE (National Marriage Guidance Council).** 76a, New Cavendish St, London W1M 7LB

UNIT THREE – FURTHER AFIELD

- **Help the Aged.** St James Walk, London EC1R OBE
- **Leonard Cheshire Foundation.** 26-29, Maunsel St, London SW1P 2QN
- **Christians at work.** 148, Railway Terrace, Rugby, Warwickshire CV21 3HN
- **Church Action for the Unemployed.** 318, St Paul's Rd, London N1 2LF
- **Cyrenians.** 13, Wincheap, Canterbury, Kent CT1 3TB
- **PHAB.** Tavistock House North, Tavistock Sq, London WC1H 9HX
- **Royal Association for Disability and Rehabilitation.** 25, Mortimer St, London W1N 8AD
- **Royal National Institute for the Blind.** 224, Great Portland St, London W1N 6AA

- **The Salvation Army.** 101, Queen Victoria St, London EC4P 4EP
- **Shelter.** 157, Waterloo Rd, London SE1 8UU

UNIT FOUR – LAW AND ORDER

- **NACRO.** 169, Clapham Rd, London SW9 0PU
- **Radical Alternatives to Prison.** BMC Box 4842, London WC1N 3XX

UNIT FIVE – ADDICTIONS

- **Alcoholics Anonymous.** See local telephone directory
- **Institute for the Study of Drug Dependency.** 14, Hatton Place, Hatton Gardens, London EC1N 8ND
- **Churches Council on Alcohol and Drugs.** 4, Southampton Row, London WC1B 4AA
- **Westminster Advisory Centre on Alcohol and Drugs.** 38, Ebury St, London SW1W OLU

UNIT SIX – PREJUDICE AND DISCRIMINATION

- **Central American Information Service.** 1, Amwell St, London EC1R 1UL
- **Commission for Racial Equality.** Elliott House, 10-12, Allington St, London. SW1E 5EH
- **Institute of Race Relations.** 247, Pentonville Rd, London N1
- **Martin Luther King Memorial Trust.** 13, Hildreth St, London SW12 9RQ

UNIT SEVEN – MATTERS OF LIFE AND DEATH

- **CARA (Care and Resources for people affected by AIDS/HIV).** 178, Lancaster Rd, London W11 1QU
- **EXIT (Voluntary Euthanasia Society).** 13, Prince of Wales Terrace, London W8 5PG
- **Family Planning Information Service.** 27-35, Mortimer St, London W1N 7RJ
- **Terrence Higgins Trust.** 52-54 Grays Inn Rd, London W1X 8JU

- **LIFE.** Life House, Newbold Terrace, Royal Leamington Spa CV32 4EA
- **National Adoption Society.** Hooper Cottage, Kimberley Rd, Off Willesden Lane, London NW6
- **Samaritans.** 17, Uxbridge Rd, Slough SL1 1SN
- **Society for Protection of Unborn Child (SPUC).** 7, Tufton St, Westminster, London SW1P 3QN
- **St Joseph's Hospice.** Mare St, London E8 4SA

UNIT EIGHT – HUMAN RIGHTS

- **Action by Christians Against Torture (ACT).** 32, Wentworth Hills, Wembley, Middlesex HA9 9SG.
- **Amnesty International.** 99-109, Roseberry Ave, London EC1R 4RE
- **Catholic Children's Society.** 73, St Charles Sq, London W10 6EJ
- **Church of England Children's Society.** Old Town Hall, Kennington Rd, London SE11
- **Dr Barnardo Homes.** Barkingside, Essex IG6 1QC

UNIT NINE – WAR AND PEACE

- **Campaign for Nuclear Disarmament.** 162, Holloway Rd, London N7 8DQ
- **Pax Christi.** St Francis of Assissi Centre, Pottery Lane, London W11 4NQ

- **Peace Pledge Union.** Dick Sheppard House, 6, Ensleigh St, London WC1H ODX
- **Quakers (Society of Friends).** Friends House, Euston Rd, London NW1 2BJ
- **United Nations Association.** 3, Whitehall Court, London SW1A 2EL

UNIT TEN – A FRAGILE WORLD

- **Catholic Agency for Overseas Development (CAFOD).** 21a, Soho Sq, London W1V 6NR
- **Christian Aid.** PO Box 1, London SW9 8BH
- **Church Missionary Society.** 157, Waterloo Rd, London SE1, 8UU
- **Friends of the Earth.** 26-28, Underwood St, London N1 7JQ
- **Marine Conservation Society.** 9, Gloucester Rd, Ross-on-Wye, Herefordshire HR9 5BU
- **Oxfam.** 274, Banbury Rd, Oxford OX2 7DZ
- **Save the Children Fund.** 17, Grove Lane, London SE5 8RD
- **Tear Fund.** 11, Station Rd, Teddington, Middlesex TW11 8QE
- **UNICEF.** 55-56, Lincolns Inn Fields, London WC2A 3NB
- **World Health Organisation.** 20, Avenue Appia, Geneva

INDEX